TECHNOLOGY
for DEVELOPING NATIONS

RUTHERFORD M. POATS

TECHNOLOGY
for DEVELOPING NATIONS

New Directions for U.S. Technical Assistance

THE BROOKINGS INSTITUTION
Washington, D.C.

Copyright © 1972 by
THE BROOKINGS INSTITUTION
1775 Massachusetts Avenue, N.W., Washington, D.C. 20036

Library of Congress Cataloging in Publication Data:

Poats, Rutherford M
   Technology for developing nations.
   Includes bibliographical references.
   1. Technical assistance, American.   I. Title.
HC60.P555   309.2′233′73   72-145
ISBN 0-8157-7118-5

Foreword

Congressional soul-searching and exhaustive studies in the executive branch have brought U.S. foreign assistance programs under closer scrutiny than ever before in their twenty-year history. During the early 1970s the aid programs administered by the United Nations and its agencies also have undergone reappraisal and change. A common theme of these reviews is the quest for better ways to harness technology to human, natural, and capital resources in low-income countries in order to stimulate economic progress.

An encouraging start has been made in the worldwide adaptation of new, high-yielding varieties of rice and wheat; this brought about the so-called green revolution and won converts to the idea that technical assistance ought to be based largely on applied research. Holders of this view reason that if the rewards of technological innovation could be extended beyond agriculture, the prospects for the very poor two-thirds of the world's people in Asia, Africa, and Latin America might be substantially improved.

This study is an inquiry into how that possibility can be realized. It does not deal with foreign-aid levels or rationales, but rather with the more practical question of how to make U.S. foreign aid more effective. It rests on the author's belief that social and technological institutions in both the developed and less developed countries should be brought together in a common systematic, problem-solving effort, in which American research and development capacities, both public and private, are linked with those of international institutions and of the developing countries. The author assesses the potential benefits of institutional collaboration and technological innovation in agriculture, industrial growth and employment, health care, population control, nutrition, and education. In his view, wider recognition of such benefits could revive public interest in international development and define a realistic and sustainable role for the United States.

Rutherford M. Poats wrote this book in 1970–71 during his tenure as a Brookings federal executive fellow. He brought to his research nine years of experience in directing U.S. foreign assistance programs, including three years (1967–70) as deputy administrator of the Agency for International Development. Previously he reported on economic and political events in Asia as a United Press International correspondent and Tokyo bureau chief. He is the author of a history of the Korean war, *Decision in Korea* (1954).

Mr. Poats wishes to thank the members of informal advisory panels of specialists in universities, foundations, and U.S. government agencies who reviewed each chapter of the manuscript. He is especially grateful to Henry Owen, director of Foreign Policy Studies at the Brookings Institution, for many helpful criticisms and suggestions, and to John A. Hannah, administrator of the Agency for International Development, whose support and encouragement made this study possible.

He also thanks those who contributed suggestions and source material: Joel Bernstein, Ernest Stern, Erven Long, Lee Howard, R. T. Ravenholt, O. J. Kelley, Martin Forman, John Hilliard, and Glenn Schweitzer of AID; Sterling Wortman, John M. Weir, and John Maier of the Rockefeller Foundation; Oscar Harkavy and Lowell S. Hardin of the Ford Foundation; Robert E. Asher, Alan Berg, and Edward R. Fried of

the Brookings Institution; Richard Dodson of the American
Council on Education; Jack Baranson and Duncan Ballantine
of the World Bank; Carl E. Taylor of the Johns Hopkins Uni-
versity; John C. Cutler of the University of Pittsburgh; Ronald
Freedman of the University of Michigan; D. Woods Thomas
of Purdue University; Thomas H. Weller of Harvard University; Philip R. Lee of the University of California; Nevin S.
Scrimshaw of the Massachusetts Institute of Technology; H.
F. Robinson of the University of Georgia; Benjamin Barg of
the UN Office of Science and Technology; Roberto Rueda-
Williamson of the Pan American Health Organization; C.
Arnold Anderson of the University of Chicago; Nyle C. Brady
of Cornell University; Robert d'A. Shaw of the Overseas De-
velopment Council; William Eilers and Julien Engel of the
National Academy of Sciences; and Lyle Schertz and Dana
Dalrymple of the U.S. Department of Agriculture. Alice M.
Carroll edited the manuscript, and the index was prepared by
Joan C. Culver.

The views expressed in the following pages are, of course,
the author's own and should not be attributed to the trustees,
officers, or other staff members of the Brookings Institution or
to the author's former employer, the Agency for International
Development.

KERMIT GORDON
President

June 1972
Washington, D.C.

Contents

Tables

Figure

CHAPTER ONE

New Opportunities
and a New Commitment

A SPATE of blue ribbon commission reports momentarily returned the case for international development cooperation to public policy agendas on the eve of the 1970s.[1] The United Nations launched with little-noticed speeches and strategy papers a Second Development Decade. Within months it was clear that the flurry of papers was not rekindling American enthusiasm for leadership in a global campaign against poverty.

The times were not propitious. The American people, in the main, were not interested in a commitment to international development on the scale and at a tempo commensurate with the needs. Their mood was turning inward, responding to newly realized domestic problems and the weary frustration of Vietnam but also reflecting disappointments in other foreign fields. Political events in several countries that had been major recipients of U.S. aid again were refuting the unrealistic notion that aid and development might assure uninterrupted

1. President's General Advisory Committee on Foreign Assistance Programs, *Development Assistance in the New Administration* (Government Printing Office, 1968); International Bank for Reconstruction and Development, *Partners in Development*, Report of the Commission on International Development, Lester B. Pearson, chairman (Praeger, 1969); Task Force on International Development, *U.S. Foreign Assistance in the 1970s: A New Approach*, Report to the President (Government Printing Office, 1970).

progress toward a world of progressive, democratic, and congenial partners of the United States.

After Vietnam, it was said, there might be a better climate for restoring national cohesion and taking a longer view of national purposes and priorities. Many congressmen suggested that both Vietnam and the 1972 elections should be settled before considering fundamental changes in U.S. participation in international development.

There may never be an ideal moment for a conclusive debate to resolve the scale and forms of U.S. roles in development assistance for this decade. Nor is there any assurance that a debate centered on the time-worn issues of "why" and "how much" foreign aid will usher in a new era of constructive internationalism.

What is more likely to make a difference in the lives of the world's poor majority is greater public and official attention to the "how" of development cooperation—how to make it work better, how to engage the world's best talents and the available public and private capital in more effective programs for social and economic progress. Better results should build stronger public and congressional support for more adequate appropriations.

There is no better time than now to take this practical step toward a broad renaissance in U.S. development assistance. The need is urgent, and two decades of experience point the way to sensible reforms. Unprecedented waves of job seekers, in the vanguard of surging population growth, are adding a new dimension to the already towering problems of the less developed countries. A pace of development that seemed ambitious in the 1960s is woefully inadequate now to meet rising demand for jobs, food, and social services in much of Asia, Africa, and Latin America. The goals of development in the 1970s must be raised both qualitatively and quantitatively to provide more employment opportunities and better health, diets, and education for vastly more people.

Yet, in all of the low-income countries, some or all of the essential resources for faster progress—natural resources, capital, and strategic human skills—will continue to be critically scarce even with the best conceivable domestic economic mobilization and international cooperation. How to ease this binding constraint is the central issue for development assistance.

Major contributions can be made by *technical* assistance in helping to design and adapt technological and social innovations that stretch available resources and create new ones. This has been the core of the technical assistance concept from the beginnings of international development cooperation, and it has been reaffirmed in the latest reappraisals. It is not a glib prescription for uncritically following the technological paths of the Western nations. Rather, it is a systematic effort to adapt technologies and the social organizations for using them to local factors and cultural values.

Neither this nor any other grand idea is the single, sufficient solution to the problems of mass poverty. Socially committed national leadership, local capital formation, and capital transfers from abroad are among other essential ingredients. But it is clearer now than ever before that no lasting solutions to the development problems of low-income countries can be achieved without continuous technological and social innovation grounded in research and experience.

Heightened international research and development efforts to realize the promise of technology figured prominently in the development policy papers that ushered in the Second Development Decade. This was also the dominant theme of plans for a permanent and more professional U.S. technical assistance system. Similar goals were suggested in studies by the

World Bank, some of the regional banks, the Organization for
Economic Cooperation and Development (OECD), and the
Canadian and other national aid programs around the turn of
the decade.

Is this renewed enthusiasm for technique-sharing and problem-solving research just another fleeting vogue? Is it likely to
be an overcorrection for past neglect that will fragment development efforts? Is the yearning of poor countries for a share in
technological miracles a flight from the hard realities of economic and social reform? Are these countries now ready, and
are the best research capacities of the technically advanced
countries now available, for more effective collaboration if the
right arrangements are made?

Most of the evidence suggests reassuring answers. The
studies underlying the new approaches to technical assistance
and the words and actions of leaders in many developing countries reflect much greater understanding of the requirements of
development than in the early 1960s. The pool of experienced
professional manpower for coping with the technical and
managerial problems has been greatly enlarged. The tools of
analysis have been refined. While the commitment to humane
development goals may be weak in some countries, political
evolution is forcing the ruling elites to accept the imperative
of social reform along with economic and technological measures.

This study attempts to show where and how U.S. technical
assistance has been and can be highly effective. It explores specific opportunities for action—in pushing back the threat of
famine, in reducing the burdens of malnutrition and disease,
in creating jobs, in bringing the promise of education closer to
reality, in curbing runaway population growth. Its focus is on
promising new directions in technical assistance, using research, research-based experimental projects, and new networks
of international professional cooperation to build problem-

solving capacities in the developing countries. Technical assistance alone is not enough, however; only rarely can it achieve lasting results if the financial or political ingredients of development are weak or misconceived. Technological and related social change often cannot start and seldom can go far without the support of other forces. There is, however, much greater scope today than in the past for practical technical and social innovations that will stretch available resources, realize more of the latent potentials of human and natural resources, and work more directly on the problems of bypassed millions in the developing countries.

Two decades of experience should have removed any sense of easy optimism or any parochial claims to "the" keys to progress. Technical assistance is not synonymous with development or even with applying technological and social innovations in developing countries. It is a catalyst and vital support to a process that must be rooted in the commitment and insights of each country's leadership elements, the attitudes and skills of its people, its natural and financial resources, its economic and policy environment, and the diverse private and public institutions that channel human effort. Since development must be home grown, the process is globally uneven. There can be no made-in-America global strategy, but the United States now can concentrate on those needs and requests it is best equipped to serve.

Some Concepts and Definitions

In the early years of technical assistance, no one fully perceived what complex and interdependent changes were implied by those deceptively simple-sounding generalizations, "technology" and "social innovation." In a broad sense, technology means "knowledge systematically applied to practical tasks." This knowledge usually grows out of analysis and discovery through research in both the natural and social sciences. To be applied to serve human needs, technology must be embodied through invention and innovation in goods and processes or techniques. Innovation is used here to mean any set of technological and social (including managerial) changes by which resources are put to more effective use. Both invention and diffusion are usually implied in this single shorthand term.

Technology and innovation refer not just to goods and processes employed by industry but also to those used in agriculture, commerce, transportation, communications, health care and protection, food science and processing, fertility control, education, and administration.

Technological change has become recognized[2] as a vital force—in a sense the greatest resource—in the progress of modern nations. Kindleberger calls it "a prime mover in the course of economic development."[3] Schumpeter says that "development consists primarily in employing existing resources in a different way, in doing new things with them, irrespective of whether these resources increase or not."[4] Technology does, of course, multiply the effective availability of usable resources, both natural and human. Long points out: "At any given time, prevailing technology defines the limit of any society's ability to command the resources at its disposal to the service of human ends. . . . Petroleum was no effective resource without the

2. Recognized very early—about 1726—by Jonathan Swift in *Gulliver's Travels*: "And he gave it for his opinion, that whoever could make two ears of corn, or two blades of grass to grow upon a spot of ground where only one grew before, would deserve better of mankind, and do more essential service to his country, than the whole race of politicians put together."

3. Charles P. Kindleberger, *Economic Development* (McGraw-Hill, 1958), p. 91.

4. J. A. Schumpeter, *The Theory of Economic Development* (Harvard University Press, 1949), p. 68.

technology of, principally, the internal combustion engine. Arid fertile lands await irrigation technology before being of value; soil is a fixed stock resource until conservation technology makes it continuously renewable; vast areas of the world are wastelands until medical technology makes them safe for human habitation, or until agricultural technology makes hostile soils, climate or salt water supportive of human life."[5]

Quinn puts technology at the center of development in concluding, "Technology is the vital growth component in each of the four traditional economic input factors: land, labor, capital and education."[6] Technological change creates new options and expanding horizons, new market forces, new social problems as well as blessings.

Social innovation is a broader process than technological innovation, including all means of adapting to current needs the organization of human activity. Technical assistance is concerned with both forms. Many other external factors influence these changes in developing countries, of course. They include political and economic competition; self-financed transfers of knowledge through education, dissemination of publications and other communications, and advisory and consultant services; trade, investment, capital loans and grants; and spontaneous imitation.

Technical assistance is a deliberate effort by public service institutions to reduce a developing country's human and technical disadvantages—as distinguished from its immediate capital shortages—in the planning, designing, and execution of

5. Erven J. Long, "Research Functions of the International Development Institute" (staff paper, Agency for International Development, 1970; processed).

6. James B. Quinn, "Scientific and Technical Strategy at the National and Major Enterprise Level," in United Nations Educational, Scientific and Cultural Organization, *The Role of Science and Technology in Economic Development* (Paris: UNESCO, 1970), Chap. 4.

social or technological changes. In the process it may influence a country's basic values and goals, but that seldom can be an explicit aim of multilateral or government-to-government technical assistance. Its concern is largely with people in the mass, but it works through a relatively small group of strategically placed leaders, institutions, and management systems in the developing countries. Technical assistance works best when it is directed at key problems identified by a coherent national development strategy that brings to bear fiscal, financial, and political tools as well as technical instruments.

The Renaissance in Technical Assistance

The initial gropings for the right roads to development during the 1950s were directed down blind alleys by simplistic "know-how, show-how" interpretations of President Truman's Point Four idea.[7] Too many believed, or acted as if they believed, that the United States could transfer the knowledge, techniques, and some of the equipment of its development to the diverse ecologies of Asia, Africa, and Latin America with little or no research and adaptation. Naïve optimism was followed by disillusionment and demands for other keys to instant, visible progress. This spawned new schools of "quick-fix" theories and programs. The slower route through research, experiment, evaluation, and institution building won little favor in the political echelons of most developing countries.

The early failure to see the dimensions of the purely economic needs of these countries led to overcompensating corrections in U.S. approaches to development assistance. Internal

7. Prior to the global Point Four program, the United States conducted technical assistance in Latin America during the 1940s through Nelson Rockefeller's Institute of Inter-American Affairs, an arm of the State Department.

savings and international capital transfusions became the overriding concern, with technology subsumed vaguely and social services left largely to parochial, independent specialists. Compartmentalized bureaucratic structures in both the aid-giving and aid-receiving countries discouraged integrated approaches to problems. A destructive dichotomy in both U.S. and multilateral aid programs soon developed between the champions of capital-oriented aid and the proponents of direct action on the human variables.

The consolidation of U.S. aid in the 1960s under the Agency for International Development (AID) was designed to help correct these tendencies. AID was designed to integrate thought and action on all the interdependent factors in U.S. development assistance. This sensible reform fell short of expectations. Too much faith was placed in strong economic growth—which did occur in many countries—and national economic plans to improve the lives of disadvantaged elements within changing societies. While there were many bright exceptions, particularly in financial and fiscal fields, AID tended to downgrade technical and social issues and the staffs representing these interests. The agency's managers became preoccupied with comprehensive country programming, the conditioning, provision, and policing of capital assistance, a host of congressional and balance of payments strictures, and a hobbling annual budgetary process. It was not the best climate for the painstaking and long-term approaches required in building institutions or attacking technological problems.

Equally important, most of the developing countries presented little demand or opportunity for international collaboration on truly innovative approaches to their problems. Their preoccupation with immediate issues and the expansion of conventional public services allowed little attention to finding better ways of coping with future problems. What research capacity they had was typically isolated from markets or public service operations. The traditional insularity of their higher education limited the applicability of the driblets of research it produced. Their patchwork of stability-oriented economic policies tended to discourage rather than stimulate entrepreneurial drive in agriculture or industry to raise productivity through socially rational technological changes. A tendency among their public officials toward superior-class detachment from the problems of the masses discouraged radical reform of health and education services.

The recitation of negatives could be extended to the point of despair. This would be misleading, because despite all the faults of governments and aid agencies there was unprecedented progress on many development fronts in the 1960s. Experience and formal learning steadily improved comprehension and capacity in both the developing countries and aid agencies. Doctrinaire theories gave way in most of the newly independent nations to pragmatic appreciation of the roles of private initiative and public policy. The sheer mass of human misery and arithmetical projections of future problems demanded and got attention, at least to the point of more thorough analysis. Better systems to use available skills evolved. The capacity of most of the large and some of the small countries to plot their own courses of development and work at a professional level with foreign experts and institutions improved fairly steadily during the 1960s. By 1970 the political imperative of a more collaborative style in technical assistance relationships had become generally more practicable as well.

Pressures for change in U.S. technical assistance programs stemmed from three main sources during the late 1960s. One was the rediscovery that concentrated and well-managed applied research can create or adapt technologies of enormous value to the less developed countries. The most striking evidence came from the Rockefeller-Ford agricultural research programs. In making possible at least the beginnings of a "green revolution," they renewed faith in technology as a means of injecting dynamism into agrarian societies. At the same time, new technologies were enabling and inspiring developing countries to launch family planning programs; but limitations in their effectiveness showed the urgent need for more research on both the social and biomedical aspects of fertility control. In this new atmosphere, aid administrators became more responsive to the long-standing complaint of the organized science community that AID neglected science and technology.

A second major pressure for change came from members of the U.S. Congress, who insisted that there must be better ways of assuring popular participation in development and a broader sharing of its fruits. They criticized—and often overstated—AID's reliance on the "trickle down" of benefits to the disadvantaged masses. In this they were supported by American youth influenced by the pessimism of the "new left," who questioned the purposes of U.S. aid programs that supported aggregate economic growth in countries where little was being done to reduce social and economic disparities among their people. One reflection of this dissatisfaction was the congressional action creating a small U.S. foundation to provide support to private social reform efforts in Latin America. Another was the revival of emphasis in the general U.S. aid programs on measures to improve "the quality of life of people."

New facts of international life constituted the third major force for change. The developing countries had acquired greater confidence (and, in varying degree, competence) in planning and executing their own programs. They also could now choose from a wider array of alternative sources for development policy advice, capital, and technical forms of aid. International organizations, in which the developing nations had a voice and where political sensitivities of the aid relationship were minimized, had become more able (although not always eager) to grasp the prickly political and economic issues of development policy. These new realities were compatible with the judgment of the Nixon administration in 1969–70 that it was time for a less activist and visible U.S. government role in the affairs of Latin America, Asia, and Africa. According to the new policy, the United States would not shirk its responsibilities as the richest and most powerful nation, but it would be less interventionist, more responsive to the developing countries' own prescriptions and requests, more interested in collaboration through multilateral and private channels.

Principles of a New Approach

The commencement of a new decade and the end of the bipolar era in world history provided a logical occasion to realign U.S. policies and roles in international development. Drawing on the recommendations of a public advisory committee of distinguished citizens led by Rudolph A. Peterson and on other reports, the administration proposed a wholesale reorganization of U.S. foreign assistance and a progressively increasing reliance on multilateral institutions. It proposed a sharp separation of U.S. development assistance from security programs and the creation of two development agencies, a capital-lending International Development Corporation and a technical assistance agency, to be called the U.S. International Development Institute.

Like most reorganization schemes, this one would pay a price for expected net gains. The separation of capital assistance and technical assistance would sacrifice the greatest potential advantage of AID programs over the traditional UN and World Bank programs—that is, the possibility of melding all forms of development assistance in concerted support of a developing country's attack on a key problem. Such sectoral efforts require far larger amounts of money and things than technical assistance programs, as usually defined, can provide. They require integrated application of human and financial resources against a common strategy and work plan.

The administration proposed to minimize this weakness by designing a set of coordinating and interlocking relations between the two agencies for technical and capital assistance. If these would work, technical assistance might have the financial dimensions to meet the real needs. However it may be achieved bureaucratically, some form of mutually reinforcing technical and capital assistance packages addressed to major sectoral problems is essential.

Other reorganization schemes designed by nonofficial groups maintained a consolidated capital and technical assistance management but included many of the substantive policy changes advocated by the Peterson task force.

Whatever the ultimate legislative, organizational, and fiscal decisions, U.S. technical assistance was moving into a new phase. The changes were a response to generally recognized needs and new opportunities.

The new approach will require establishment of a relatively permanent system of U.S. technical cooperation with developing nations, designed to make a more direct impact on the quality of lives of their people and to raise the efficiency of their use of resources. This goal must be pursued through sustained efforts, employing the most competent U.S. talent from whatever source, to build the capacity of developing countries and international institutions to solve key problems. The program should make greater use of the United States' greatest relative strength, its science and applied technology, not to build technological societies but to provide technological aids to social innovation. The whole program should be infused with the methods of applied research, and the research and development capacities of developing countries should be selectively strengthened, both directly and through goal-directed research projects addressed to key economic and social problems.

In this kind of program, U.S. technical assistance can be concentrated on activities where the requests and needs of developing countries match actually available and superior U.S. capacity to help and on innovative work that promises to multiply benefits or produce "ripple effects." The program will offer greater scope for use of professional intermediaries (grantees, contractors, or individual experts drawn from other public agencies or private organizations), attract broader participation by professional associations, promote long-term collaborative relationships, and reduce the U.S. government's direct involvement.

The key terms for the new approach are "innovative," "research based," "collaborative," and "selective." These principles, or some of them, can be found in the best U.S. technical assistance practice of the past. The primary models, however, are the research-intensive international programs of the major private foundations.

The new approach has won enthusiastic endorsement from professional communities. To prove its case by performance to the larger U.S. public and the Congress will take years. Yet it requires from the outset a congressional assurance of long-term authorization and flexibility. The program's increased emphasis on research and research-based experimental projects also demands new attitudes on the part of both the Congress and technical assistance managers. The Congress traditionally has restricted research in the AID budget. The fact that technological and social innovation is dependent on research, experiment, and evaluation has never been widely understood within AID and therefore not persuasively expressed in executive branch presentations to the Congress.

The case for research can be made abstractly. It also can be drawn from visible evidence of both the brilliant use and shameful neglect of research in the technology-based economic progress and environmental troubles of wealthy countries. The case for more systematic methods of using research and building it into operations in developing countries can be understood best in the light of the great human problems facing these countries.

This study examines those common problems in each of six major sectors addressed by technical assistance and suggests means of improving present approaches to problem solving. Its immediate aim is to provide practical insights on how to improve research management, how to make greater use of research capacities of both the advanced and developing countries through joint efforts, and more broadly, how to raise the effectiveness of international technical cooperation. Its larger objective is to outline an agenda for action and contribute to a renewed zest for constructive international cooperation by Americans.

CHAPTER TWO

Agricultural Research: The Infinite Frontier

SCIENTIFIC AGRICULTURE promises to produce—in fact it must produce—the greatest technical achievements of twentieth century man. The economic and social advances made possible by agricultural technology in the United States, Western Europe, and Japan during the first half of the century must be surpassed in the less developed countries. Their agriculture must outrun unprecedented population growth and become an accelerator of general income and employment gains.

The prime task of development in most of the poor countries is to invigorate their rural economies. More than two-thirds of the people of the less developed nations as a whole depend directly on agriculture for employment. In the 1960s agricultural products accounted for one-half to two-thirds of the export earnings of all these countries, except the major mineral exporters and a few that reached a stage of rapid industrialization. Agriculture and to a minor extent fisheries provide these countries' only dependable defense against future famines and their primary means of overcoming the current diseases of malnutrition and undernourishment. Low incomes in traditional agriculture are the greatest drag on overall development in most of the countries of Asia, Africa, and Latin America.

Until the late 1960s agriculture showed little promise of becoming an invigorating force for general economic and social progress in "traditional" societies. Direct transfers of Western technology to their agrarian systems had failed to accelerate growth in personal income and capital formation or to trigger advances in industry, services, and social welfare. Real income growth, for the mass of rural people, was at best glacial. Food production, while rising at a historically satisfactory rate of about 2.7 percent annually, was barely keeping ahead of population growth. It was falling behind effective food demand and even further behind requirements for adequate nutrition.

Population projections illuminated the longer term dimensions of the problem, and severe droughts in southern Asia in 1965–66 cast it in harsh and immediate terms. The less developed countries (exclusive of communist nations) would at 1960s growth rates add more than 1 billion people to their populations between 1962 and 1985. The rising proportions of young and urban people would radically shift the demands on farm families:[1]

Item	1962	1975	1985
Total population (millions)	1,394	1,948	2,514
Farm population (millions)	935	1,175	1,388
Arable acres per farm family	7.2	5.7	4.9
Nonfarm consumers per farm family	2.7	4.9	4.1

By 1985 the developing countries would need nearly two-and-one-half times as much food as in 1962, one-third of that increase resulting from modest annual gains in their very low income levels. If their rate of agricultural production did not increase, they would have to import an inconceivable $40 billion worth of food annually by 1985.[2] In human terms, mil-

1. United Nations, Food and Agriculture Organization, *A Strategy for Plenty: The Indicative World Plan for Agricultural Development* (Rome: FAO, 1970), p. 5.
2. Ibid., p. 33.

lions of victims would automatically be added to the hundreds of millions suffering from nutritional diseases if their demands were not met. Periodic declines in food production would raise prices and impose further disadvantages on the low-income majority. The projected expansion in new job seekers could not be absorbed without a radical increase in overall economic growth, and much of this faster growth would have to rest on a more dynamic agricultural sector.

The pace of agricultural growth in the 1960s was danger-ously inadequate:[3]

| Year | *Growth index (1961–65 average = 100)* | |
	Total food production	*Food production per capita*
1961	94	99
1962	97	99
1963	101	101
1964	104	101
1965	104	99
1966	106	97
1967	111	100
1968	115	101
1969	120	103
1970	124	103

A panel of experts, convened by the Science Advisory Com-mittee to the President of the United States to consider the problem, recommended comprehensive measures to raise the annual growth rate in food production in the developing coun-tries to an unprecedented 4 percent and to sustain that rate for twenty years.[4] (This would require greatly expanding buying

3. Interview, Charles Gibbons, Economic Research Service, U.S. De-partment of Agriculture, March 1971. Figures for 1970 are preliminary crop reports.

4. President's Science Advisory Committee, *The World Food Problem,* Report to the President (Government Printing Office, 1967), Vol. 1, p. 22.

power and popular knowledge of nutrition as well as modernizing agricultural production.) The UN Food and Agriculture Organization (FAO) set an overall target of 3.7 percent annual increase in agricultural production that called for crop and livestock growth rates of 3.9 percent in Asia, 3.4 percent in sub-Sahara Africa, 3.3 percent in Latin America, and 3.7 percent in the Near East and northwest Africa.[5]

As the Indian droughts of 1965 and 1966 led to predictions of massive famine by 1975, the world was awakened to the necessity of getting agriculture moving.

Seeds of Hope

Help, fortunately, was at hand for a significant portion of the food-deficit areas. For much of the rest, there was at least hope of technical solutions if science, economics, and politics could apply the lessons of a limited success on a global scale. A readily available potential for help existed in the often maligned agricultural institutions of the developing countries that had developed during the years of technical assistance. The most striking factor was new: a quantum jump in the production of irrigated wheat and rice, using high-yielding varieties of these basic cereals.

The first of the "miracle" seeds were introduced in 1964–65 by the two international research institutes established by the Rockefeller and Ford Foundations, the International Maize and Wheat Improvement Center (CIMMYT) in Mexico and the International Rice Research Institute (IRRI) in the Philippines. Lineal descendants of the CIMMYT and IRRI wheat and rice varieties were quickly developed by national research centers in India and elsewhere—in some cases with

5. FAO, A Strategy for Plenty.

help from the foundations and aid agencies. About the same time, a high-yielding corn variety was developed in East Africa through collaboration of U.S. Department of Agriculture scientists (supported by the Agency for International Development [AID]) and African plant breeders.

The new seeds were an explosive force. They released energies few had believed to be present in the supposedly tradition-bound villages and agricultural extension agencies. They offered farmers something they could not ignore, a twofold or better increase in yields. They gave previously ineffectual extension services a package of highly productive technology to extend. They challenged local research stations to similar and more urgent achievement. They awakened political and financial authorities in food-deficit countries and the international assistance community to the great potential returns on well-managed research investments.

Where the seeds could be successfully grown, they produced unaccustomed marketable surpluses, demanding public and private investment in marketing and transportation systems. They created cash incomes for subsistence farming villages, stimulating demand for sewing machines, bicycles, and many other light industrial goods. They required unprecedented investments in fertilizer, pesticides, and, in some places, water pumps and wells. These new capital and operating costs sparked demand for rural credit, particularly to serve small farmers.

The new technology required more labor as well as capital. Double, and in some cases triple, cropping became technically possible and economically attractive where water and other growing conditions permitted. This extended demand for farm labor throughout the year. (Over the longer run, of course, as productivity outran market demand, farm labor would be displaced.)

As with other innovations, those farmers who could raise

cash or dared to plunge into debt gained income advantages over less favored or less daring neighbors. Those who had access to irrigation gained production advantages. As the output of the early adopters of the new technology rose, breaks occurred in grain price levels. Government intervention became necessary in some places to protect the late or less efficient adopters and to help some shift into other crops.

The ultimate social and political impact of what William S. Gaud, then administrator of AID, named the "green revolution" is not yet predictable. Government action, especially to preserve or expand small-unit farming, can ameliorate the more dangerous social possibilities. In order to assure broad human progress, however, social policy measures must accompany technological innovation.

As important as were these initial achievements of agricultural science, they were just a beginning. But what a beginning! Some 30 million acres, in addition to 1.9 million acres already established in Mexico, were planted in the high-yielding new varieties of wheat or rice by their fourth year of general release. By 1969, the fifth year, the total was about 44 million acres—about one-fourth of the wheat acreage and over 10 percent of the rice acreage of the Asian and African countries that were able to shift to the new technology.[6] Small farmers as well as the "big" men of the villages adopted the new seeds and practices at a pace comparable to the switch to hybrid corn in the United States. The technological innovations therefore made possible a wide sharing of the billions of dollars of increased farm income.

For the vast majority of farmers in the less developed countries, however, nothing has changed. Perhaps 10 percent of the land devoted to cereal grains in all of these countries combined

6. Dana G. Dalrymple, "Imports and Plantings of High-Yielding Varieties of Wheat and Rice in the Less Developed Nations" (Department of Agriculture, 1971; processed).

could use the new seeds available in 1970. What has been done ought in some measure to be reproducible for the benefit of the left-out majority. If so, agriculture can become a dynamic force for general economic progress in a much larger part of the developing world. The FAO estimated that with continual introduction of locally adapted new varieties, high-yielding technology can be applied on one-third of the cereals acreage of the developing countries by 1985. These hopes rest on a multitude of decisions and commitments by the world community, by governments, aid agencies, scientists, and farmers.

The Achievements

The spectacular beginning was the result of timely and well-organized research. It is important to learn the right lessons from this achievement.

The trigger was radically—not marginally—improved technology, a set of precisely determined production practices for use of distinctly superior semidwarf grain varieties that could grow at varying latitudes, mature rapidly (especially in the case of rice), and convert water and large amounts of fertilizer into grain rather than additional stalk and leaves. The research involved large-scale screening of germ plasm banks, painstaking genetic engineering, and systematic testing of new breeds under varying conditions to find the best combinations for yield, harvesting, processing, and taste appeal.

The research was directed toward explicit goals. Rockefeller Foundation scientists leading interdisciplinary teams of experts from several nations had an assigned mission: to achieve a breakthrough of major proportions in actual on-farm productivity. Their objective was not simply to produce new knowledge about rice and wheat or produce new varieties that agricultural agencies might or might not choose to examine and adopt. It was to produce seeds so profitable that they would bring about a significant reduction of the food deficit and to help interested countries get and adapt the technology for prompt use.

This method achieved phenomenal returns on research investments and won a 1970 Nobel Prize for the chief geneticist of the wheat program, Norman E. Borlaug. When he accepted the award he said of the joint research effort: "We never waited for perfection in varieties or methods but used the best available each year and modified them as further improvements came to hand. This simple principle is too often disregarded by scientific perfectionists who spend a lifetime searching for the unattainable in biological perfection and consequently during a lifetime of frustration contribute nothing to increasing food production."[7]

From the outset, provision was made for adaptive work in each interested country. The new rice and wheat varieties were not expected to be the last step in the process of creating the best seeds for each locale. The initial releases carried genetic resistance to some, but by no means all, of the mutations of disease organisms and insects that afflict these crops. Long-term and widespread dependence on inherited defenses would surely invite catastrophic crop losses. In fact, both the IRRI rice seeds and the CIMMYT wheat seeds soon were afflicted by locally virulent diseases in some countries. IRRI and CIMMYT brought agricultural scientists from these countries into the centers as senior staff members, on-the-job trainees, or visitors. All took back to their home research stations the infectious zeal, methodology, and promising seed materials of the international centers. At home, they launched their own parallel research, crossing the new seed materials with estab-

7. Norman E. Borlaug, acceptance speech at Nobel Prize ceremony, Oslo, 1970.

lished local varieties. As a consequence, India, Pakistan, Malaysia, Ceylon, and the Philippines were ready to complete local trials of the IRRI and CIMMYT seeds soon after they were released by the centers. Shortly thereafter, they were ready to issue their own modifications of these seeds.

The momentum of this critically important adaptive work in each rice and wheat producing country must be maintained indefinitely. Greater genetic diversity must be bred into future generations of seeds to guard against wholesale epidemics of plant disease and insect scourges.

The research job has only begun. The rainfed areas of South Asia, the Middle East, and North Africa do not have high-yielding wheat, nor the tropical uplands of Latin America a high-yielding rice variety. Disease resistance must be strengthened in rice seeds for irrigated agriculture everywhere. Corn breeding, a more difficult task, is moving slowly, and the tailoring of grain legumes, root crops, and pasture grasses to the ecologies of the less developed nations is even further away from realization. Work has only recently begun on combining high-yield and high-protein genetic traits in the basic food crops.

Research must be intensified on the multitude of special problems posed by cultivation of the humid tropical lowlands, where most of the unused fallow land is to be found. Equally pressing is training and research in economics to guide individual farmers and agricultural strategists in choosing policy and practices. Marketing research is needed to extend the benefits of success in production. The list is long.

The Strategic Setting

By the end of the 1960s, development leaders were ready to heed the call for a more systematic and research-grounded attack on agricultural problems. Experience had confirmed the contentions of expert studies. An influential report to the President of the United States in 1967 had outlined a two-part effort for the country:

First, in its dealings with the developing countries, the United States should help educate and orient their leaders to the critical need for long-range research and educational programs. In jointly sponsored economic development projects, the United States should make certain that adequate financial support is given to these programs. Further, it should use its influence with international and regional development banks and credit agencies to encourage loans for facilities and equipment needed to carry on food-related research and educational projects.

Second, the United States must greatly increase its own commitment to food-related research and educational programs. This can be done only if there is a national recognition of the long-term nature of the world food supply problems and the need for massive and continuous efforts to solve them. With appropriate long-term commitments, U.S. universities, government agencies, foundations and industry can make research and educational contributions far in excess of the efforts of the past.[8]

A thread common to this report and subsequent studies provides direction for U.S. agricultural assistance in the 1970s. The central necessity for a better world is an improved food–population balance in the less developed countries. Food production must be expanded and population growth rates moderated simultaneously. Agricultural growth (including animal and fish farming) in the less developed countries is urgently required because most of these countries cannot afford to meet their future needs through imports and probably will not be able to control population growth rapidly enough to close food gaps.

Diversified food production and qualitative improvement in

8. Science Advisory Committee, *The World Food Problem*, Vol. 2, p. 634.

basic food crops can reduce nutritional problems. The traditional avenue to increased food production, through opening new lands to cultivation, is today a significant possibility only in parts of Latin America and Africa, and is only a medium-term expedient of undetermined cost. Land-saving agricultural technology can trigger overall economic and social progress, especially when designed and managed to benefit small-unit cultivation; however, longer term advances depend on comprehensive development of industry, education, health services, and transportation.

Scientific agriculture requires comprehensive, continuous, production-oriented research and training. Since most adaptive or applied research must be adjusted to local conditions, national and regional research stations in developing countries must carry out the work of determining complete packages of materials and practices to fit particular settings. Local research must be linked closely with advanced agricultural education and graduates must be imbued with a sense of community responsibility.

These principles are now widely accepted. Pursuit of them raises a long list of questions for policy makers and operators of the developing countries and assistance agencies. What can be done with limited means, limited skills, and scant leadership to build the more effective systems of national research and training needed right now? How can foreign experts, advisers, and financial resources best be used? How can foreign technology be analyzed, selected, and adapted to local conditions most efficiently? Should basic research be left to the rich countries and international centers?

Should local universities or agricultural colleges be expected to take on the additional burden of conducting essential agricultural research, in view of their inability to staff their classrooms adequately? Should agricultural research and higher education be fully integrated, or loosely associated, with extension services? What connection should they have with a national research council? What are the prime research targets, and what is the best system for fixing and changing priorities? What proportion of the national research program should go to support of individual scientists' initiatives and how much to directed research programs?

Once a new, high-yielding technology takes hold, policy makers face new or intensified problems that must be solved by economic and social research. How should production and rural employment objectives be reconciled? When increased agricultural productivity pushes production past demand, how far can output prices decline without reducing agricultural per capita income, ruining less efficient producers, or increasing labor surpluses? What are the means and costs of protecting the smaller or less advantaged farmers, supporting prices until demand catches up, stimulating urban and export demand, shifting production to other crops? In such a volatile situation, how can rates of return on irrigation, fertilizer plants, and other major investments be projected over amortization periods?

Assistance agencies face such problems as how to incorporate practical research content into technical aid programs and how to incorporate training and institution-building into research programs.

These problems of development administration can be sorted out under three broad headings: means of setting research targets or priorities; designs for research management systems; and international collaboration in research and training. The categories overlap. For example, setting priorities is a function of research management; training, like research, should be guided by output objectives and relate to the systems of management in which graduates are to work.

Research Priorities

The potential range of research in agricultural technology is almost boundless. It can encompass literally hundreds of thousands of distinguishable plants and animals, from giant trees to microscopic organisms. At the center of life are the green plants, which convert the sun's energy into forms usable by all other living things. Agricultural history suggests that about 3,000 of the roughly 350,000 plant species described by botanists have at one time or another been tried as food sources. Only a dozen now provide, directly or indirectly, 90 percent of the world's food supplies. Fifteen account for all of today's important food crops: rice, wheat, corn, sorghum, barley, sugarcane, sugarbeet, potato, sweet potato, cassava, common bean, soybean, peanut, coconut, and banana. "The tendency through the centuries has been to use fewer and fewer species and to concentrate on the more efficient ones, those that give man the greatest return for his land and labor."[9] This concentration also can be traced to accidents of history, born of cultural taboos and social practices, and to the lack of means to harvest, process, transport, or protect alternative food crops.

Three-fourths of man's food comes, directly or indirectly, from the cereal grasses. Cereals adapt to a great diversity of climatic, soil, and water conditions. They are well suited to mechanization, and as dehydrated food they are easy to handle, store, and transport with a minimum of processing. With urbanization, their advantages are magnified. These common food crops produced and processed in various environments

9. Paul C. Mangelsdorf, "Genetic Potentials for Increasing Yields of Food Crops and Animals" (paper prepared for symposium on Prospects for the World Food Supply, National Academy of Sciences, Washington, 1966; processed).

must be the main focus of agricultural research for developing countries.[10]

The vast array of little-utilized plants in the humid tropics has for years been a tempting frontier for agricultural research. Most of these leafy plants, however, have seemed on close examination to be difficult to harvest, to provide a low ratio of consumable food to byproducts, or to require costly processing to fit into prevailing human food or animal food practices.

Most experts see great promise in the genetic improvement of the traditional cereals, grain legumes, tubers, and meat animals, making them more efficient converters of nutrients into human food, less susceptible to diseases and pests, more adaptable to diverse climates, easier to control and harvest. A relatively new target is the development of higher concentrations of proteins or limiting amino acids in these basic food crops.

A more venturesome research goal is the endowment of the major cereals with the legumes' capacity to restore soil fertility through fixation of atmospheric nitrogen. If cereals could be made even partially efficient imitators of the legumes, the cost of food production would be enormously reduced.[11]

Some of the greatest accomplishments of agricultural research have been in plant and animal health measures—devising defenses against rodents, insects, fungi, bacteria, and other pathogens. Salvation of U.S. crops from their natural enemies has produced high economic returns for organized agricultural science.[12] Pests and pathogens destroy or frustrate the produc-

10. Glenn W. Burton, "Food Resources in the Plant Kingdom," in *The Food Resources of Mankind*, a Symposium sponsored by McDonald College, McGill University (Montreal: Agri-World Press, 1968).

11. J. George Harrar, *Strategy for the Conquest of Hunger* (New York: Rockefeller Foundation, 1967), p. 58.

12. Albert H. Moseman, *Building Agricultural Research Systems in the Developing Nations* (New York: Agricultural Development Council, 1970), pp. 39–40.

tion of more than 100 million tons of food crops annually. They exact huge tolls of domesticated animals, forest timber, and fresh water fish. The human tragedies caused by these enemies of the farmer are immeasureable; the payoff from successfully applied protective research is only partially measured in the billions of dollars worth of crops saved.

The costs of technological advance, in widely distributing powerful insecticides and other chemical agents that upset the natural ecological balance, are becoming apparent. Protective research should be turned toward breeding into food plants stronger biological resistance to diseases and insects. This is not a new concept. "Genes for resistance to powdery mildew from wild American grapes saved the grape industry of France before the turn of the century. The watermelon industry of the [U.S.] South was saved by transferring genes for resistance from the inedible citron melon to the wilt-susceptible edible types. These genes that protect crops against disease in the United States make an annual contribution to our economy in excess of $1.5 billion."[13]

Agricultural research must include work on soils and water. Extension services in most developing countries know little about soil and water management. Except for a few tropical export crops most of the accumulated knowledge has been produced in temperate zone countries and is not fully applicable to tropical food production. Tropical and subtropical areas need massive public and private investments in irrigation; more efficient use of existing irrigation facilities; wide dissemination of better techniques of land leveling, drainage, and cropping practices to conserve water and maintain soil permeability; measures to guard against and reverse soil salinity; fertilizers tailored to the heavily leached soil in the high-rainfall

13. Burton, "Food Resources in the Plant Kingdom."

tropics; and means of increasing natural nitrogen fixation in the upland tropics.

Agricultural research also encompasses forestry and tree crops, aquaculture, and aspects of economics, chemistry, mechanical engineering, and food science. At one end of the spectrum it merges with chemistry and biology, at the other with human nutrition, industrial technology, and sociology. Each branch of research offers exciting challenges to the specialist and difficult budgetary choices for the agricultural development manager.

The bewildering array of choices is one of many problems in setting priorities. In any developing country the expertise and facilities to carry out useful research are limited. Their available talent is largely the product of academic training, with little or no experience in the practical application of agricultural science. Their university-based scientists work in educational and incentive systems that incline them toward theoretical teaching and, at best, part-time research aimed more at publication than at production. Departmental insularity discourages the practice of group research by interdisciplinary teams in both universities and public research institutions. National development planning tends to slight the technological aspects of agricultural development. Political interests sometimes impose special enthusiasms or preconceptions on research managers. And—universally—budgets are pathetically inadequate.

That the capacity for agricultural research has not been nurtured can be partially blamed on the foreign aid agencies. Over the past ten to twenty years they have trained agricultural graduates, helped establish agricultural schools and extension services, and offered advice on agricultural strategy. But only in exceptional cases have they emphasized research or made a sufficiently sustained, imaginative effort to bring all the components of a national agricultural science system together in effective working collaboration.

Nor have the potential contributions of agricultural modernization to national development been carefully explored. Wisely applied agricultural research and development can contribute directly to industry by lowering the real cost of raw materials, and indirectly by increasing rural incomes and demand for goods, capital formation, and expansion of export earnings or import-substitution. It offers the mixed blessing of releasing less efficiently utilized manpower from marginal farming to industry, services, and nonfarm agribusiness at the same time that it stimulates, at varying rates, the demand for employees in these sectors.

Analysis of key agricultural problems and opportunities in a number of countries and experience in international programs have provided the basis for judging the most urgent agricultural tasks for international research collaboration. Repeatedly in their judgments of regional and global priorities for agricultural research, experts stress development or adaptation of high-yielding and high-quality grain legumes, sorghums, tropical root crops, and rainfed wheat and rice varieties that would extend the green revolution.[14] Expressed or implied is the necessity of continuing protective research. More intense work is recommended on tropical livestock, tropical soils, and water management and on an array of farm management problems either integral to or independent of development of high-yielding seed strains. In tropical countries with significant potential export markets for fruits and vegetables, research on these crops is also stressed.

Most of the experts tend to relegate agricultural economics research to a supporting role or to integrate it with compre-

14. See Appendix for the priorities recommended by a number of experts.

hensive work on each technically defined priority. One dissenter cites a host of social science research tasks, including pricing, marketing, fiscal, and other economic and social matters, that should be undertaken independently of physical research. He does not view these policy fields as so politically sensitive as to preclude outside participation in reasearch. He urges that investment primarily support the national research needs and capabilities of the less developed countries.[15]

Certainly it would be wrong to build a new U.S. technical assistance program, or even a network of international agricultural research centers, on a static list of a half-dozen research priorities. To do so would ignore the great diversity of needs and aspirations among more than a hundred developing countries and the continual emergence of new opportunities arising out of new knowledge. The United States should concentrate its program on a few fairly common problems whose solution it is most interested in and capable of contributing to; the United States should not, however, confuse its special interests with the spectrum of research priorities.

Research Management Systems

While the economic returns on successful research can be enormous, time, talent, and money can be wasted if traditional research patterns are accepted. How research is organized and linked to its markets—that is, research management—is too important a question to leave entirely to the fraternity of scientists.

Management is a rarely used word in the literature on agricultural research. It seems to be shunned as incompatible with scientific inquiry. Indeed, it can be overdone; there is a place

15. Letter to the author from D. Woods Thomas (Purdue University), September 1970.

for unprogrammed, pure scientific investigation. But only a well-designed management system linking research, extension services, and policy offers much hope of focusing and accelerating efforts to solve urgent agricultural problems.

In this sense, efficiency is low in the traditional agricultural research and extension efforts of the less developed countries. Their research programs typically have consisted of driblets of effort, sometimes duplicating work already done elsewhere, seldom addressing concurrently all the obstacles to more profitable production, frequently divorced from the practices of "dirt farming." While lip service is paid to the necessary link between research and extension services and of both of these to training and economic policy, the bureaucratic walls between these interdependent functions are more pronounced than their operational linkages. Attempts to overcome this insularity and irrelevance by bringing research budgets under the control of national research councils have been helpful, but often these councils occupy themselves with awarding grants or parceling out budgets rather than producing and directing an agricultural research strategy.

There are outstanding exceptions to this discouraging picture. Mexico's and Taiwan's major crop research and extension programs and the recent food crop campaigns in India, Pakistan, and the Philippines showed encouraging innovations in the coordination of all the service institutions to obtain production results from new technology.

If agricultural research is to produce high returns, it must in one expert's view be:

(a) directed against all technical barriers to productivity of a given commodity, with clear national production and farm-level yield targets;

(b) led by highly competent and dedicated scientists, with major responsibility assigned to one individual for sufficient years to obtain measurable results;

(c) conducted by inter-disciplinary teams of scientists capable of simultaneously attacking all major problems; and

(d) adequately supported with both men and money, so that results from central experiment stations can be widely tested and promoted on farms.[16]

(All of this can fail, of course, if the product of the research is not distinctly profitable to the farmer.)

These criteria, developed from the overseas experiences of the Rockefeller Foundation and the successes of the U.S. agricultural programs, imply close integration of extension and research systems. Extension services must at least be given substantive guidance by scientist-leaders of the national agricultural research system. The research scientist thus must be able and willing to undertake the "necessary experimentation, testing, and demonstration on farms in each locality to be served." All the personnel of the combined services "must be trained in the essentials of technical agriculture at the central or regional experiment stations, capable of demonstrating to uneducated farmers, of diagnosing and prescribing remedies on the spot. Success must be measured in impact on agricultural output."[17]

The U.S. model extended to less developed countries suggests a network consisting of a major national research center, a number of smaller regional or specialized stations, and many local verification and testing stations, the latter integrated with local extension or production services to farmers. One advocate with wide experience in the United States and overseas argues that the U.S. system is workable for small as well as large countries on whatever scale they need and can afford.[18]

16. Sterling Wortman, "The Technological Basis for Intensified Agriculture," in *Proceedings of a Conference on Agricultural Development*, Bellagio, Italy (New York: Rockefeller Foundation, 1969).

17. Ibid.

18. Moseman, *Building Agricultural Research Systems*.

It is one matter to advocate a locally feasible variant of the three-tiered research network linked intimately with farm-level production advisory services. It is quite another to try to graft the U.S. system of agricultural education, research, extension, and related agribusiness onto a society with radically different educational levels and governance, limited private business services, and no traditions of research management. Foreign advisers and national agricultural leaders in developing countries should concentrate on the fundamental goal of closely linked training-research-production services and work continually to bring the possible closer to the desirable.

The essential conditions for an agricultural research program in each country as seen by another specialist are:

First, it must be *comprehensive*, since relatively little is gained by changing only a variety, or a fertilizer, or a plant production practice, or a farm implement. These are complementary factors that usually need to be simultaneously and jointly considered within the research program itself. Second, it should be *continuous*, partly because the strains and populations of disease organisms keep changing, and partly because the sets of farm practices that may be new today are always far from the best that man can achieve, and even more productive practices are going to be needed in a very imminent tomorrow. Third, it should be *widespread*, because soils, moisture, climatic factors and prices vary so much from one farming locality to another.[19]

Another would pursue the goal of an integrated "national research, training and production system" through:

—ambitious but technically feasible goals for both production (by commodity) and farmer involvement;

—functioning interdisciplinary teams at major experiment stations, capable of handling all problems of each important commodity, with smaller teams at regional stations, and with production specialists trained in testing and demonstration at the farm level;

—continuous, competent scientific leadership;

19. Agricultural Development Council, *Report for 1967* (New York: ADC, 1967).

—integrated involvement of colleges of agriculture and the Ministry of Agriculture;

—serious efforts to reach the small farmer;

—in-service training of substantial numbers of production specialists (extension agents);

—research and training focused on high-priority problems— "directed" research, carefully guided by well-informed leaders who must insist that the national interest not be neglected; and

—close association with appropriate international centers and international projects.[20]

The best of the agricultural service systems in the less developed countries fall short—probably many years short—of achieving this ideal design. Foreign assistance can help to improve the national agricultural services in nations that have committed themselves to clear goals.

From this survey of priorities and organization, some general guidelines for agricultural research and development managers may be distilled:

• Technological research on either export or domestic food crop improvement should be planned and managed to achieve production goals, not stopping with new knowledge. It must include the design and introduction of necessary production practices and assure on-farm testing at real costs. This will be a radical departure in most developing countries. It necessitates close integration of research and overall development programs. It requires collaboration with other key services. It forces adoption of team approaches to finding and removing all the technical and social barriers to increased production of a particular crop in a coordinated effort. It sets a standard of economic feasibility or profitability in actual farm application of the new technology produced by a research program.

• In countries experiencing or facing over the next decade significant food deficits, agricultural research should sharply focus on improving the efficiency of production of basic foods im-

20. Wortman, "The Technological Basis for Intensified Agriculture."

portant in the eating habits of the mass of their people. This does not preclude diversification, but it does assign low priority to work on food crops likely to have a market limited to a small fraction of the populace. In some countries, for example, it will mean low priority for meat production research.

• Collaborative research should be aimed at improving the nutritional quality of basic food crops. This is a very promising means of raising general dietary and health standards. Advanced countries and international centers can do most of the original research, and national research establishments of the less developed countries can undertake the local adaptation of improved varieties.

• Research on the agricultural utilization of natural resources, such as soils and water, should be oriented toward real production problems; it should be integrated into research on specific crop or animal production practice at the earliest practicable stages.

• Nonbiological research in farm management, land tenure reform, economic incentives and social policy, marketing, storage, processing, transport, and so forth, also should be addressed to issues raised by particular new technology or crop campaigns. Social science need not be subordinated to technological research, but experience suggests that it is more likely to find ways of adapting technology to local environments when it is part of productivity-oriented programs in developing countries.

• Programs must provide for continuous follow-on research to maintain and protect advances in seed strains and techniques against the certain onslaught of new or adapted disease organisms, insects, or market changes. The underlying principle should be that agricultural research is a permanent and expanding function of national development.

These guidelines allow for diversity of research goals and measures for increasing production in individual countries.

Their application, however, would tend to impose an economic discipline on programs and reduce to manageable proportions the variety of research activities claiming limited resources. They thereby also serve to concentrate the field of collaboration and assistance from foreign aid agencies and the international agricultural science community.

International Collaboration and Assistance

If the demand for food, jobs, and social progress were less urgent, the normal processes of development, reinforced by traditional aid and professional interchange, would be sufficient to bring about effective agricultural research and production services in most of the developing countries. The demand is urgent, however, and the time required to meet it will, at best, be painfully long. Business-as-usual will not be tolerable.

This business must be carried out largely in the developing countries and by their people. This is true of most of the research work and higher education as well as of the extension services. It is more obviously true of the social and economic policy analysis and institutional changes affecting agricultural land tenure, income distribution, mechanization, and marketing. The upgrading, energizing, and focusing of these public services to agriculture is, quite literally, a life-or-death matter for most of the developing nations.

Fortunately, international cooperation, if designed to do so, can be crucially helpful and politically acceptable in this field. The reorganization of the U.S. foreign assistance program and concurrent efforts to modernize the UN development programs and other national aid programs provide a rare opportunity to institute a more effective system of agricultural development cooperation. (While outside the scope of this study, important elements of such a system are large-scale assistance to overall development and more liberal trade treatment of the agricultural exports of developing countries.) A more effective system of international technical cooperation should be grounded in these principles:

• Investment in manpower to solve agricultural problems must be commensurate with agriculture's critical importance and complexity. Strengthening the educational and research capabilities of developing countries is of first importance, but this is not enough. If the quality of technical assistance is to rise, better ways must be devised for attracting superior U.S. professional experts and institutions to this work. Basic to this objective is putting U.S. technical cooperation on a relatively permanent basis, with long-term program commitments and a research orientation in most activities. Through financial assurance for their operation, a greater variety of organizations should be developed for mobilizing U.S. technological and social science manpower for both short- and long-term service —in developing countries, in special international programs, and at their home bases.

• Operational assistance should be concentrated on a few key production and employment goals in a national agricultural strategy. A crop campaign or an area development program backed by national political leaders often provides a good vehicle for engaging local and foreign experts and institutions in joint analysis of problems that would go unattended or fall between the stools in routine government operations. Special campaigns or programs also offer opportunities to mobilize staffs of local universities and research centers to work on real-life issues, to the benefit of both the operational programs and the academic institutions.

Technical assistance agencies must become more flexible to make a comprehensive campaign or program work. They must be willing to make their foreign technicians integral staff members of regular and ad hoc organizations of developing countries. They may need to provide budget support for local costs to assure that a critical element of a program does not bog down. Aid donors must be willing to commingle their resources and sacrifice their identification with a particular project when a large program requires pooling of resources. Local leaders must assume greater responsibility for promptly reconciling policy issues and for coordinating various national and local agencies and international helpers interested in all aspects of their programs.

• Agricultural science must be mobilized everywhere and in every practical way to raise production efficiency in the developing countries. Financing of applied research should be radically increased in Asia, Africa, and Latin America. Agricultural science should be given a central role in development programs and emphasis shifted to production-oriented, directed research. The long-term projects of aid agencies, especially those concerned with training institutions, should have a research orientation and, where needed, operational staffing for research should be supplied.

Professional collaboration among agricultural scientists and institutions in the developing and developed nations should be more systematically organized. The rudimentary elements of an international network for research collaboration have long existed. They include journals on agricultural research, international seminars such as those arranged by the FAO, the foundations or specialized professional organizations, overseas research projects jointly supported by aid agencies and local universities, export crop industry research and development, and personal collaboration among individual scientists.

A more structured system, organized and directed at priority needs, is now evolving. It should include arrangements to guard against overcentralization of judgments and controls. Enthusiasm for the strictly international aspects of the system is a constant threat to the less glamorous, more disorderly business of strengthening the national elements. Increasing the capacity and stimulating the performance of research, training, and production services *in the developing countries* should be the primary objective of an international agricultural science network.

International Centers

The four international agricultural research centers already established by the Rockefeller and Ford Foundations are the most prominent elements of the new network. They have brought together a critical mass of outstanding scientists from many disciplines and countries to help fill the production technology gap as quickly as possible and to train national research and extension scientists.

The international centers were conceived as a means of facilitating a free exchange of scientists, ideas, breeding materials, and methodology among countries concerned with a common agricultural problem. Their private, apolitical character would enable them to employ outstanding scientists of the developing countries and engage them in technical assistance to neighboring countries without some of the psychological problems of accepting aid from another less developed country. They were not designed "to replace national efforts but rather to supplement them and to facilitate the development of national capabilities."[21] Their internal operation, it was suggested, should not receive more than 10 or 15 percent of international financial support for agricultural research.

The successes of IRRI and CIMMYT were more than the production of high-yielding rice and wheat varieties. Those

21. Will M. Myers, "The Place of the International Research Centers in the Network" (paper presented at a conference of international program directors, National Association of State Universities and Land Grant Colleges, Urbana, Ill., 1970; processed).

institutes also challenged the research and extension services of developing countries to better performance, trained some of their key staff, and provided timely on-site technical advice in several countries. The newer centers—the International Center for Tropical Agriculture (CIAT) in Colombia and the International Institute of Tropical Agriculture (IITA) in Nigeria—did not initially have the same, possibly critical, strength of concentration on one or two crops. IITA plans included work on corn, soybeans and cowpeas, cassava, sweet potato, yams, forage grasses, and legumes, as well as rice. Its overriding mission, however, is to find feasible alternatives to the shifting culture now widely practiced in the tropics—to determine how land can economically be farmed without turning it back to forest for ten to fifteen years out of each cycle. CIAT research goals cover soil and crop practices in the lateritic soils of the lowland, humid tropics; tropical livestock production and related forage and pasturage, animal nutrition, and health; and crop work covering rice, corn, grain legumes, and root crops. The four institutes are similar, however, in their methods of exchanging staff, information, and breeding materials with existing national and international agencies.

By becoming a regular financial contributor to the support of the four centers, AID sought to assure that the centers fulfill their great potential as training and technical assistance resources for national development. Within the limits of their regional and crop specialization, they can logically take on a much greater share of the country-based technical assistance work performed by the contract teams and regular staff of the UN and national aid agencies. Given sufficient funds, they can employ the best talent of whatever nationality in a completely professional relationship with developing country institutions.

With AID financial support, IRRI has provided assistance to rice research in several Asian countries. The UN Development Program helped to fund CIMMYT's search for high-protein wheat. The FAO, under its Middle East wheat and barley improvement project, sent crop scientists of that region to CIMMYT for research training. CIMMYT also has collaborated with the new Canadian International Development Research Center in research on triticale, a cross of wheat and rye for dryland farming. The Inter-American Development Bank has made grants to CIMMYT and CIAT to train Latin American researchers and production specialists.

"If properly organized and managed," according to an independent observer, "such international centers will probably provide the greatest output/input ratio of any method of organizing our research efforts. These centers will likely be more successful in the development of new varieties of not only the crops currently under investigation but others as well . . . through intensified breeding efforts which will likely be possible only at international centers of various kinds."[22]

Encouraged by the interest of some of the official aid agencies, the Ford and Rockefeller Foundations and the Canadian International Development Research Center began early in 1970 analyzing the need for additional research and training thrusts: in grain legumes; in water management for crop production; in livestock diseases of East Africa; in upland crops under conditions of natural rainfall; and in agricultural economic and social policy management. Other subjects that may be researched effectively in an international center or international cooperative program include starchy root crops, oilseeds and pulses, and livestock production in Southeast Asia. Any new centers, like the present four, would have international staffs and boards of directors representing the host countries and major financial contributors.

The World Bank, UN Development Program, and FAO

22. Letter to the author from Nyle C. Brady, June 1970.

have taken the lead in establishing a consultative group of assistance agencies to assure financial support for the existing and new international and regional centers, including extension of their technical assistance activities in the developing countries. A technical advisory committee, in which the developing countries are strongly represented, screens proposals for the consultative group.

Coordinated International Research Programs

Another promising new element of the international network is the association of centers of specialized competence—research stations or universities—of the developed and less developed countries in multisite work on a single major agricultural problem under the leadership of a preeminent institution. This differs from conventional scientific collaboration largely in the coordinating or directive role of the lead institution or scientist. The leader provides the research materials such as seed plasm or basic research findings, technical advice, and where necessary supplemental staff to the cooperating institutions. Through consultation among the members, the leader gets agreement on a comprehensive research design and on allocation of the work. He sets uniform reporting standards and facilitates exchange of information with the world community.

Few existing programs combine all these characteristics of directed research, but several should evolve in the ideal direction. Among the most complex and potentially rewarding is the international hybrid wheat program, which aims to create new, high-yielding strains with 15 to 25 percent more protein and markedly higher levels of wheat's most limiting amino acid, lysine. The program originated in an AID-financed search by University of Nebraska scientists for high-protein germ plasm among the 15,000 bread wheats of the U.S. Department of Agriculture's world wheat collection. It has evolved into a two-headed collaborative scheme, with Nebraska scientists guiding a plant-breeding effort in more than two dozen countries on winter wheats and CIMMYT leading multisite research on spring wheats. The FAO has helped to arrange international cooperation in the programs.

Other collaborative arrangements that might be strengthened and accelerated include international sorghum and high-protein corn programs (supported by AID) led by Purdue University and engaging the collaboration of institutions in major growing areas around the world; Inter-Asian corn improvement and East African maize improvement programs (supported by CIMMYT, the Rockefeller Foundation, and AID); Inter-American potato improvement (supported by CIMMYT) and swine improvement projects (led by CIAT); a Middle East wheat and barley improvement project (supported by FAO with CIMMYT assistance); and international weed control research (led by Oregon State University and involving centers in two Latin American countries with AID support).

The fish-farming research of Auburn University may be suitable for this kind of international collaboration. A variety of realistic verification trials in several countries may be arranged through such collaboration to test the phenomenal yields of nine tons of edible fish per acre at Auburn. (This is two-and-one-half times the efficiency of poultry production in transforming feed to meat.)

Coordinated international programs on serious plant and animal protection problems affecting several regions also seem likely to yield complete solutions more quickly than would conventional, independent research.

These collaborative research programs are relatively inexpensive. They rely on existing facilities of the participating institutions rather than requiring a new central station. Because researchers are picked on the basis of demonstrated personal or institutional competence and remain most of the time at their home bases, the likelihood of engaging the full- or part-time services of the best experts increases. The normal financial resources of the cooperating institutions cover many of the costs of the program in each country. A sponsoring aid agency, dealing directly with the cooperating institutions or only through the lead institution, provides the financial support required for the additional work involved in the collaborative research plan.

The collaborative plan should include training and field applications. Senior scientific staff should be exchanged among the cooperating institutions and internships should be set up for graduate students of the cooperating institutions (or of universities associated with a cooperating research center). An important objective of the research scheme should be to lure agricultural education out of the classroom and into the experiment stations and farms of the less developed countries. It also should achieve some side benefits in propagating better research methods.

The opportunities for participation by Japanese, European, and other centers of specialized excellence in coordinated multinational research schemes is a further argument in their favor. Partly because of language difficulties, Japan's highly successful experience in directed agricultural research has not been extensively tapped. Many small European research centers and centers established in former colonial territories could make useful contributions in specialized fields.

Regional Centers

A third potential element of the network is regional and subregional agricultural research and training centers sponsored by intergovernmental organizations in Latin America, Asia, and Africa. Such centers would seem to be particularly useful to small countries that will not for many years be able to afford full-fledged national research systems.

This appealing concept has serious drawbacks. With very few exceptions, existing regional organizations cannot assure long-term financial support of major new undertakings. Finance and agriculture ministries of the participating countries prefer to spend national funds on strictly national development programs. Furthermore, the regional centers do not have direct access to or control over member nations' experiment stations and extension services, where research findings must be tested and put to use. If they must work through technical assistance arrangements, traditional jealousy or pride may prompt officials and scientists in the receiving country to reject the advice of a team of neighboring-country experts. If the regional center is dependent on outside governments or agencies for annual aid donations, its future may remain insecure and its staffing consequently a notch below that which the foundation-linked centers can attract.

All these problems do not arise in all cases, and they may be surmounted where they do. The East African Agriculture and Forestry Research Organization and the Inter-American Institute for Agricultural Sciences in Costa Rica seem to have overcome most of the problems of regional centers. Nevertheless, proponents of regional centers must bear the burden of proof that they offer the best way of meeting an unsatisfied need for research and training.

Information System

An improved network of agricultural science needs a high-speed, reliable information system. The conventional means of professional communication provide coverage that is neither complete nor timely, especially with respect to research planned or underway.

The great majority of the world's agricultural research activities will remain outside the systems of international collaboration financed by foreign assistance. This valuable capacity should not be ignored in planning the mobilization of science for agricultural development.

The international community should provide, at little or no cost to members of the agricultural research fraternity, current reports on all significant findings, activity, and planning affecting any part of the network. The FAO appears to be best suited to undertake global responsibility in this respect. The other components of the network—the international centers, regional centers, and collaborative programs—would have built-in means of information exchange.

Summary

Systematic, sustained action to stimulate agriculture in the less developed countries is a compelling necessity, not just to prevent hunger but also to inject dynamism into the whole process of economic and social development. Agriculture must be made capable of absorbing some of the rapidly growing labor forces, opening markets for industrial and service growth, and generating capital for new investment. Somnolent, traditional agriculture, coupled with excessive population growth, will condemn the majority of mankind to a future of deepening frustration.

This is a problem for a world community, and the means of dealing with it include virtually every form of international peaceful collaboration—in trade, investment, banking, education, health, social analysis, and technology. Among all concerned the resources exist for greatly improving the agricultural outlook of most of the low-income nations.

Here is a particularly exciting challenge to a nascent international community of agricultural development scientists and specialists in agricultural economics, sociology, and natural sciences. They have the capacity, if properly organized and supported by financial and trade measures, to turn the promise of a green revolution into reality for much of the world. Most of this capacity is not engaged effectively today.

Recent limited successes suggest more effective ways of mobilizing professional expertise for agricultural development. New forms of international collaboration in research, education, and large-scale innovative programs will be needed. They require a long-term commitment to international collaboration by universities, research centers, specialized private organizations, foundations, and government agencies.

In the United States, support and, when appropriate, leadership for the new approaches must come from a wide variety of experts and organizations outside the staff of the aid agency. Nongovernmental organizations and individuals must initiate collaborative programs with people and institutions in the developing countries, and the U.S. technical assistance agency can then offer support. Advisory panels and other means of mutual stimulation among official and private organizations will help to make the system work.

The indispensable requirement is this nation's commitment to cooperation in agricultural development as a part of its international relations from now on.

CHAPTER THREE

Mobilizing Technology
for Industrial Growth

IN THE 1970s the politics and economics of the developing nations converge on this question: Where will millions of redundant human beings find jobs? The problem is not new, but its newly alarming dimensions are forcing a redefinition of the minimum goals of development. Job creation is beginning to challenge per capita income growth as at least a coequal target and test of development strategies. At issue is whether and how to tilt the scales of agricultural, industrial, service, and broader policy decisions toward faster growth of employment. The challenge is to create new jobs and almost simultaneously raise productivity—to make economic progress serve more people.

The cities of countries caught in the vise of poverty and population pressure give vivid warning of the possible shape of things to come. Urban populations of the less developed countries—except for a few very dynamic economies—have lately been growing twice as fast as urban jobs. Nevertheless, the cities continue to attract more ill-equipped immigrants from backwater villages and marginal or overmechanized farms. These millions for whom the system offers only frustration dispute the comfortable statistical evidence of developmental progress. Their numbers will mount toward a critical mass of explosive potential unless workable solutions are found soon.

Minds numbed by big numbers have failed to comprehend

the prospective employment demands and their implications for industrial development and trade policy. The less developed countries (excluding Communist China) can expect about 150 million to 170 million new entrants to their labor forces in the decade of the 1970s.[1] Quite apart from reducing their present severe unemployment and underemployment, these countries must try to create productive jobs for 300,000 to 350,000 people each week in the decade. This is about 50 percent faster growth of new job seekers than in the 1960s, a decade in which unemployment rose despite generally strong economic growth in the developing countries.

If annual growth rates in gross national product (GNP) that averaged 5 percent failed to generate jobs for all who sought them in the 1960s, what rate of economic growth will be required to employ entirely outside of agriculture the much larger surge of job seekers in the 1970s? The shocking answer offered by a World Bank economist is that it will take about twice the 1960 growth rates—9 to 11 percent annually.[2] This estimate is not radically out of line with those of Raúl Prebisch and associates at the Latin American Institute for Economic and Social Planning. They calculated that an average Latin American GNP growth rising to 8 percent by the end of the 1970s and sustained in the next decade would gradually reduce underemployment in services and absorb new labor force entrants, but only if the agricultural sector retained about one-third of its own natural labor force increases.[3] An interna-

1. J. N. Ypsilantis, "World and Regional Estimates and Projections of Labor Force," ISLEP/A/VII. 4/Add. 1 (Geneva: International Labor Organization [ILO], 1966; processed).

2. S. K. Singh, "Aggregate Employment Function: Evaluation of Employment Prospects in LDCs," quoted in Robert d'A. Shaw, _Jobs and Agricultural Development_ (Washington: Overseas Development Council, 1970).

3. Raúl Prebisch, _Change and Development: Latin America's Great Task_ (Washington: Inter-American Development Bank, 1970), pp. 67–80.

tional study team found that if Colombia set out to achieve full employment, it would have to sustain annual output growth rates of about 9 percent in industry and the services and 5 percent in agriculture for fifteen years, reform its agriculture so as to retain in rural employment more than half of that sector's natural labor force increases, and deliberately reduce the recent rate of gain in labor productivity in the nonagricultural sectors.[4]

Fueling this demand for jobs is the unprecedented rate of population growth, caused by traditionally high birth rates out of phase with sharply reduced death rates. The developing countries face at least another decade of annual labor force increases of more than 2 percent in Asia and Africa and nearly 3 percent in Latin America. This is two to four times the rate of labor force expansion that the developed nations had to absorb in their nineteenth century transitions from agrarian to industrial systems. Population programs may begin to slow the rate of increase (but not the absolute numbers) of new job seekers in some countries by the early 1980s, later in other countries. For the present decade and much of the 1980s, however, the future job seekers are already born.

It would be comforting to believe that agriculture might absorb as much as it contributes to labor force growth. In some countries where small-unit farming and labor-intensive technology are encouraged and where locally adapted high-yielding crops and favorable growing conditions combine with strong demand for farm products to permit multiple cropping, agriculture may do its share in creating new direct employment. But if these conditions and policies do not obtain, or if productivity runs far ahead of demand for farm labor, the new job seekers will stream off the farms to the towns and cities. Mechanization and consolidation of farmland into larger units will accentuate agriculture's release of manpower.

4. Dudley Seers and others, *Towards Full Employment* (Geneva: ILO, 1970), pp. 51–62.

The indirect employment benefits of agricultural modernization are more promising. Sharply increased productivity generates marketable surpluses and greater earnings and savings, stimulates rural demand for both capital and consumer goods, and infuses dynamism into the entire economy. If sustained by market demand, this more productive agriculture can create jobs in rural agricultural processing industries, transportation, commerce, and an expanding circle of urban manufacturing industries. This bright promise depends on the large "if" of rising demand for farm products. And that demand depends on the vitality of the rest of the economy and export markets.

Primary reliance will continue to be on growth in nonfarming employment, but with an important difference: where the new agricultural technologies can be made to yield their benefits in capital formation and market expansion with slight or slow displacement of farm labor, industry now has a powerful booster. Increasingly more productive agriculture and industry, interacting to boost demand, also should stimulate job creation in the services sector, especially in transport, commerce, finance, and government social services.[5]

Three other factors should enhance industry's capacity to accelerate its creation of wealth and employment. One is the prospect of a global system of tariff preferences for the manufactures of the less developed countries by the developed. Another is the still fragile evolution of regional trade and industrial integration schemes among groups of developing nations. The primary importance of these measures to stimulate exports

5. South Korea reduced its unemployment rate to about 5 percent in the late 1960s with a phenomenal industrial expansion that produced about as many jobs in the services sector as in industry. At the same time, agriculture was retaining very little of its natural increase in workforce. The Korean industrial performance cannot be widely duplicated, but other countries with less growth in output might, with economic and social policies oriented toward job creation, exceed Korea's employment gains.

lies in their influence on policies and attitudes of both governments and industrial entrepreneurs in the developing nations
—causing them to take greater risks to raise production efficiency and move out into competitive markets. The third
factor of increasing significance is the shift of industrial production by big multinational corporations to plants in the developing countries, bringing technological and management
innovations as well as capital.

All of these potential boosts to industry in the developing
countries are vulnerable to sharp setbacks. At best they cannot
relieve some of the fundamental human, institutional, financial, and technological handicaps of the poor countries. They
do brighten prospects, but not enough to assure the rapid and
sustained industrial growth that an employment strategy requires.

After output growth averaging 10 percent annually in the
1950s and about 7 percent in the 1960s, the whole manufacturing sector was contributing only about 17 percent of total domestic production in the less developed noncommunist countries. (The proportions ranged from 12 percent in Africa to
about 24 percent in Latin America.)[6] Their total industrial
output was about one-twentieth that of the developed countries, and their per capita manufacturing values averaged only
about $20 compared with $600 in the developed countries.[7]
Manufacturing employed only 10–20 percent of the active
labor forces of the developing countries in the late 1960s, substantially the same proportions as in the early 1950s.[8]

Because the base is so low, seemingly important gains in industrial employment have little impact on the rising jobless-
ness or underemployment in most of the less developed coun-

6. United Nations, Industrial Development Organization (UNIDO),
Industrial Development Survey, 1970, Vol. 2, Table 7.
7. UNIDO, *General Issues of Industrial Policy* (1969), p. 78.
8. UNIDO, *Industrial Development Survey*, 1969, Vol. 1, Table 83.

TABLE 3-1. Growth of Manufacturing Output and Employment in Developing Regions, 1960–66

Item	Change from preceding year, in percent						Average annual change between 1960–63 and 1963–66, in percent
	1961	1962	1963	1964	1965	1966	
Light manufacturing							
Developing nations, total							
Output	5	3	4	7	6	5	5
Employment	4	3	5	5	2	1	4
Latin America							
Output	5	1	1	8	5	4	4
Employment	1	…	−1	5	2	5	2
Asia[a]							
Output	7	6	7	6	8	6	7
Employment	5	4	7	5	2	5	5
Heavy manufacturing							
Developing nations, total							
Output	11	5	6	11	6	7	7
Employment	5	5	4	8	5	4	5
Latin America							
Output	12	4	1	11	6	8	6
Employment	3	1	−4	9	3	7	3
Asia[a]							
Output	9	11	13	10	8	5	10
Employment	6	7	8	7	7	4	8

Source: United Nations, Industrial Development Organization, *Industrial Development Survey, 1970*, Vol. 2, p. 67.
a. Japan and communist nations not included.

tries. In the period 1960–66, jobs in industry in the developing countries as a whole rose about 4 percent annually—5 percent in Asia but only 2 percent in Latin America (see Table 3-1).[9] It would take five times these rates of labor absorption by industry in Asia and nine times in Latin America to provide direct industrial employment for all the new job seekers.

The conclusion is inescapable that industry alone cannot provide such rates of growth in direct employment widely and over the long term. In many countries, however, there is no alternative to greater reliance on industry to absorb part of the labor force increases and, more importantly, to make it possible for the services to absorb a larger proportion. This indirect contribution to job creation rises where industry is most efficient in using scarce resources to generate public and private savings.

Jobs and Technology

In the developing countries as a whole, output per worker in manufacturing increased at about 3 percent annually from the mid-1950s to mid-1960s, compared with about 4 percent in the industrialized countries.[10] In Asia, labor productivity in manufacturing rose faster between the mid-1950s and mid-1960s than in the world as a whole.[11] Productivity measured in terms of value added per worker in a sample group of developing countries (see Table 3-1) averaged about one-fourth that of the Western industrialized countries, excluding the United States, in the early 1960s.[12] Further gains in the developing

9. UNIDO, *Industrial Development Survey*, 1970, Vol. 2, Table 32. Industry is defined here as manufacturing and mining.

10. UNIDO, *Industrial Development Survey*, 1969, Vol. 1, Table 86.

11. M. M. Mehta, "Employment Aspects of Industrialization" (Bangkok: ILO, 1970; processed).

12. UNIDO, *Industrial Development Survey*, 1969, Vol. 1, p. 260.

countries' industrial labor productivity probably occurred late in the 1960s. They were sometimes bought at high cost, through subsidized investment in capital equipment.

The dilemma is the same as in agriculture: how to reconcile productivity and employment objectives. The developing nations clearly cannot afford to forgo what has historically been a prime factor in economic growth—the diffusion and application of technology, which raises the value of labor and capital. Nor can they tolerate wholesale technological unemployment. Is there a way out through invention or use of labor-intensive technology?

Economies with a surplus of labor and a shortage of capital are frequently advised to concentrate on capital-saving processes throughout industry and to expand efficient labor-intensive industries whenever possible. Each of these options depends on both a capacity to know and project real social costs and an incentive to select the right technology for economizing on the scarcest local factors of production—usually capital, skilled technicians, and production managers. Neither condition for practical application of these policies is found in most developing countries.

Development policy makers have paid lip service, sometimes excessively, to capital-saving or labor-intensive technology, but government policies and institutions have typically encouraged investment in capital-intensive processes appropriate to quite different economies. Exchange rates and preferential tariffs have made it possible for businesses to import underpriced equipment. Import-substitution policies have created protected markets where innovation is unnecessary, production often small, and creeping obsolescence a danger. Foreign aid and local development bank loans (sometimes at close to negative interest rates) have lowered investment costs for capital goods but not for labor. National research and development institutions and technical education have done little to reduce developing countries' dependence on imported technology.

The transfer of technology has often occurred under licensing agreements that specify product characteristics that only the foreign investor's capital-intensive equipment can achieve. (There have been some encouraging exceptions to this practice in the design of locally economical production processes by multinational companies.) Licensing arrangements for trademarked consumer goods sometimes expressly forbid any alteration in the production processes that might change the style or quality of the product.

Where the local entrepreneur is fully responsible for selecting or adapting technologies, he usually must employ a professional consultant who, whether local or foreign, is unlikely to have been trained to find labor-intensive innovations. Equipment salesmen reinforce the plant owner's natural urge to keep up with the Joneses, and tied loans are equally constricting. Uncertainty about the availability of spare parts may make it impossible to predict the real costs of using simpler, older types of machinery.

Nor are true labor costs easy to determine. Workers who are not well nourished, who are indifferent to machine maintenance, or who require extensive training on the job may truly be more expensive than a labor-saving machine. Shortages of skilled technicians and plant foremen may make "machine-paced" operations[13] more prudent than reliance on the initiative and judgment of plant employees to maintain production levels and quality standards. The substitution of intermediate technology in production of component parts may entail heavy use of the scarcest resource of all, process engineers and technicians; single-purpose machines, on the other hand, require

13. Albert O. Hirschman, *The Strategy of Economic Development* (Yale University Press, 1958), p. 145.

lower levels of skills to maintain and repair than complex or automated ones.[14]

In power production or chemical fertilizer production, labor intensivity is obvious nonsense, and in many other processes it proves to be an inefficient way to use capital; "given capital as the scarce factor in developing countries, the problem is not to save the use of it in the production process but rather to maximize the output which can be gotten from it."[15] Although labor-intensive technologies may produce jobs in the short run, "it is far from certain that they lead to rapid development and thus to full employment in the long term."[16] There is evidence that a number of labor-intensive industries in Asia have proved to use capital more efficiently than the capital-intensive ones; "the argument that labor-intensive industries consume more capital per unit of output, therefore, is untenable."[17] Small-scale labor-intensive industries in Korea have registered gains in both productivity and direct employment.[18] What makes sense in Korea, however, may not work in some Latin American countries where social security legislation has made labor costs relatively high.[19]

In short, the choice of technologies requires a discriminating judgment. Private and public interests often conflict, and the public policy maker seldom has clear facts to work from. Governments, development assistance agencies, and foreign investors can, however, reduce the biases against socially rational

14. Jack Baranson, *Industrial Technologies for Developing Economies* (Praeger, 1969).

15. Werner Baer and Michael E. A. Hervé, "Employment and Industrialization in Developing Countries," *Quarterly Journal of Economics*, Vol. 80 (February 1966).

16. Yves Sabolo, "Sectoral Employment Growth: The Outlook for 1980," *International Labor Review*, Vol. 100, No. 5 (November 1969).

17. Mehta, "Employment Aspects of Industrialization."

18. Ibid.

19. Joseph Grunwald, "Some Reflections on Latin American Industrialization Policy," *Journal of Political Economy*, Vol. 78, No. 4 (1970).

choice of capital-saving means of production. They should collaborate on measures to facilitate creation and adaptation of technology appropriate to each given situation. They will seldom go wrong in pressing for labor-intensive methods in construction and most services. They should not, however, adopt a slavish, indiscriminate bias toward labor intensivity in manufacturing.

The Scope for Public Action

If the pace and quality of industrial growth in developing countries are to measure up to the need for jobs, their governments and international assistance agencies must play more sophisticated roles in the industrial development process than in the past. They will have to face up to the necessity of reconciling their employment interests with other pressures in policies affecting trade, private investment, foreign exchange and tariff rates, financial markets and development banking, technology transfer, research and development, training, labor organization, and public attitudes.

Assistance in formulating economic policy and in designing financial institutions is likely to be the province of multilateral financial agencies in the 1970s as they expand their technical services in these fields. For U.S. technical assistance the major tasks in the industrial field are to help build national capabilities for technological innovation and for training managers and skilled workers for industrial operations.

In addition to formal training for industrial workers and post-secondary education programs in business and economic administration, a variety of training tools can be developed. Fellowships for overseas training of industrial managers can be provided largely by the UN Industrial Development Organization (UNIDO), by particular projects financed through private investment or capital assistance programs, and by individual donor governments. National productivity centers and international productivity associations are especially useful in offering informal or on-the-job training for industrial managers. These institutions were created largely under U.S. assistance programs beginning with the Marshall Plan and running through the early 1960s. They sponsor management workshops, seminars, and overseas observation visits; circulate industrial information; and lobby for relevant formal education in business administration. Some of the productivity centers have branched out into management consulting services and direct technical assistance to their member companies. The concept now is well established and needs only further local initiative in focusing on such commonly neglected areas as management and training systems in equipment maintenace, supply procurement, and stock control.

UNIDO is filling the need for global statistical information and analyses of industrial development trends. It also offers advice (of very uneven quality) on industrial strategy to developing countries, sometimes in association with the World Bank or specialized UN agencies—such as the Food and Agriculture Organization in the case of agricultural processing.

The U.S. technical assistance agency now can concentrate on important, relatively neglected aspects of industrial development that can be separated from general financial assistance. One area in which U.S. competence is outstanding is the management of technological innovation. The systems approach, perfected by U.S. industry and consulting firms, links market research, basic science and technology research, process and product design, and engineering in a mutually recharging circuit. The U.S. government has set the pace in national industrial standards research and services. U.S. universities have led in examining the economics of technological change and devising projection techniques to enable rapidly changing industries to make sound technological decisions. In natural resource surveys, government and university experts as well as nonprofit private organizations have devised techniques that have made their services in strong demand by developing countries.

Politically, the United States is compelled to make greater efforts to help relieve the technological handicaps of the poor countries. The charge of U.S. "technological imperialism" may be unjust, but the impatience of countries falling further behind in the industrial technology race is understandable in view of the negligible U.S. aid contributions to industrial technology programs over the past decade.

The inability of industrial companies in the developing countries to create and adapt technologies has forced governments to establish a variety of public research institutions, most of them disappointing. It also has inspired a search for workable international schemes to fill the gaps in national research capacities. The U.S. scientific community has criticized AID for neglecting industrial technology in its preoccupation with other aspects of development. The U.S. technical assistance program must be modernized, but the record of disappointments will simply increase if the science/technology cart is put before the marketing horse.

The Main Arena: Proprietary Technology

Perhaps the first step in planning public action is to face the fact that public institutions in the developing countries can make only modest contributions to the total stock of knowledge and embodied industrial technology. Private (or autonomous publicly owned) enterprise and commerce have, and are likely to continue to have, the predominant roles in creating and transferring industrial technology.

Multinational corporations are instrumental in this process because their success depends in large measure on a global capacity to apply science and technology to production and marketing. These companies are "the dominant institutions transferring industrial technologies across national borders"; they do it through sale of their goods; through training for users of their products and establishment of local service facilities; through investment in local production and training of workers and technicians; through technical assistance to local customers and to local suppliers of materials, components, or subassemblies; through introduction in their locally staffed field operations of the methodology of integrated research, development, and engineering innovation; and through influence on or example to local competitors and suppliers.[20] Not all of this makes everyone happy in countries where multinational companies have appeared on the local industrial scene, but it is one of the new facts of international life.

Less publicized but far more numerous and therefore significant in the technological modernization of the developing countries are the smaller foreign investors. They have established thousands of production facilities with much the same set of benefits and costs to their host economies as those ascribed to the large multinational corporations.

Another important channel of technology transfer is the international sale or licensing of patented designs or production processes. Such licensing arrangements have been Japan's main source of foreign technology. The ability to apply and adapt these imports and move on to further innovations has enabled the Japanese rapidly to close technological gaps and forge ahead in many fields. Despite the fact that licensing ar-

20. James B. Quinn, "Technology Transfer by Multinational Companies," *Harvard Business Review*, Vol. 47 (November–December 1969).

rangements often are encumbered by market limitations and rigid technical conditions, they are indispensable to industrial development of the late-comers.

Korea's recent surge into the ranks of major exporters of manufactured goods illustrates another kind of transfer of private technology. Some of this development has been sparked by foreign buyers who, without the niceties of patent searches and licenses, simply say to a Korean businessman something like, "Copy this and we'll both get rich." There are, naturally, no statistics on this kind of technology transfer. The foreign buyer can in many legitimate ways be a powerful force for technological innovation. He creates a market big enough to warrant investment in improved technology. He sets quality and style standards that benefit local consumers. He provides designs, arranges for acquisition of patented processes, and assists local manufacturers in setting up plant layouts or in solving packaging and other problems. The wholesale buyer may be the forgotten man in the process of technological innovation.[21]

Engineering and other technical consulting firms, international educational exchanges, scientific and technical literature, open access to patents in the public domain, and trade in producer goods are other important channels in the flow of technology.

The well-springs of this flow are the competitive pressures, taxes, and incentives that work on industrial entrepreneurs, and the innovative people they are able to recruit in technically educated societies. These advantages are multiplied when they

21. John F. Gallagher, "Markets as a Basis for Industrial Development," in *Industrial Development*, Vol. 4 of U.S. papers for UN Conference on the Application of Science and Technology for the Benefit of the Less Developed Areas (Washington: Agency for International Development, 1963), pp. 62–70.

operate in a system that links market, laboratory, and production line in a continuous circuit.[22]

In the industrialized countries the scope and diversity of the largely privately generated technology are almost infinite. The annual publication *Applied Science and Technology* covers 230 technical publications in only three countries, the United States, Britain, and Canada; its 1969 edition requires 1,456 pages simply to list the bare subject references to articles published during that year on topics ranging from ACTH and Aberration (optics) to Zwitterions. In recent years, expenditures on research and related engineering by U.S. industrial concerns have exceeded $10 billion annually, an amount greater than the national budget of any but the largest developing countries even when allowance is made for price differentials. One licensor of a relatively commonplace diesel engine series for overseas production furnished more than 3,000 pages of specifications, including 145 technical and engineering guides, 67 special manufacturing methods, 439 materials standards, 340 process standards, and 25 salvage procedures for rejected parts.[23]

National Industrial Technology Programs

The sheer magnitude of the facts of presentday industrial life and their disparities tempt developing countries to consider shutting out foreign technology, or to denounce the patent system, or to try to close the gaps through public efforts to duplicate the technical resources of the industrialized countries.

Logic would dictate a more pragmatic strategy: Developing

22. Franklin R. Root, "The Role of International Business in the Diffusion of Technological Innovation," *Economic and Business Bulletin,* Vol. 20 (Summer 1968).

23. Baranson, *Industrial Technologies for Developing Economies.*

countries should design their trade and investment policies to exploit aggressively the rich flow of technology across national boundaries. A local research and training capacity should be selectively tailored to fill those gaps in the available international stock of technologies identified by local economic and technical analysis of industrial opportunities. Economic and educational policies should nurture and evoke, rather than retard, the innovative capacities of their people. Rigorous efforts should be made to reduce hidden public subsidies in the pricing of factors of production so as to encourage selection of technologies that are socially useful.

How to follow these guidelines and avoid the dangers of "technological colonialism" without wasting resources and time on ineffectual research institutions is the tough question. Until very recently, responses to this challenge have been parochial and piecemeal. Scientists have concentrated on getting national science policy pronouncements from governments or establishing science advisory councils nominally close to the seats of govermental power. The various ministries concerned with natural resources, industry, or trade have established research and industrial service functions or obtained a little more money for existing ones. Universities have tried to exploit national concern to get more funds and students in their science and technology programs. Foreign technical assistance agencies have responded with overseas training, support for equipping or upgrading local training and research institutions, and advice from science policy consultants and resource survey teams. The United Nations has described the need for a "world plan of action" to accelerate technological progress in the lagging countries and an "infrastructure" of institutions to serve this purpose. Only rarely has any government or aid agency tried to tie these strands together and take economic and financial measures to make the technical institutions more effective.

Certainly there is no single "correct" strategy for every nation and aid agency. There are, however, some universally sensible first steps. These are to try to see the processes of industrial innovation whole and to design an industrial technology program that begins and ends in the marketplace.

The Industrial Climate

A thorough assessment of the industrial climate should expose the costs of import-substitution schemes or trade and exchange rate policies that insulate industries from competitive pressures. It may also lead to fiscal and financial inducements for industries to improve their competitive positions in export markets, to undertake more of their own technological research and adaptation, or to buy these services from public or private research and development sources.

Public Economic Institutions

In most countries, central economic planning bodies and development banks are not equipped to deal with technological factors in development. This may suggest the introduction or strengthening of techno-economic analysis staffs in these institutions.

Industrial Technical Assistance

A program that strengthens technical services to industry can help to reduce the gap between the average and best practice in an industry, a step Denison calls more promising than advancing the frontiers of knowledge.[24] In countries where private technical and management consulting services are under-

24. Edward F. Denison, *Why Growth Rates Differ* (Brookings Institution, 1967).

developed, development banks or foreign financial assistance agencies can create market demand for these services by requiring independent feasibility reports, construction supervision, and—in some cases—continuing technical assistance to operations. These loan conditions should favor local and joint-venture technical services in order to build local capacity. In the absence of private technical service firms, a national development bank or governmental agency may have to create an autonomous public subsidiary to provide assistance to small industries in technical, financial, or market studies, cost analyses, applied research on plant layout, materials-handling and equipment-maintenance systems, technical literature and patent searches, and general trouble-shooting. This public company should operate on a commercial basis with very limited government subsidy; in a market economy it should shift to partial or complete private ownership as soon as possible.

Company and Industrial Group Research

The first line of attack on industrial technology problems is ideally at the company level. There the practical needs and opportunities are best perceived and all involved feel a personal stake in the effort. Weakness in or a complete lack of company research should be a priority concern of a national industrial technology program. Changing the general economic and psychological incentives will not overcome all the human and financial obstacles to development. Even in the most industrialized countries, governmental action has been required to stimulate research, largely by permitting companies to charge off research and development expenditures against taxes. Australia has instituted a direct matching grant of government funds to companies for certain research activities. A joint study by the U.S. National Academy of Sciences and the Brazilian National Research Council recommended that businesses in Brazil be allowed tax credits in the form of operating expense deductions equal to 200 percent of their contributions to higher scientific and technical education and 150 percent of their outlays for research.[25] Another approach is to allow concessional loan terms by an official development bank to cover part of a company's research program. Cooperative programs of industrial associations, to undertake both research and employee training for members and to receive government subsidies, may be an interim solution where individual companies are too small to operate their own programs.

Government Assistance in Negotiating Foreign Technology Agreements

A clear understanding of the preponderant role of international trade and investment in the transfer of technological knowledge should lead governments to change the focus of their interventions in the negotiation of foreign investment or licensing agreements. One of the keys to Japan's industrial achievements has been its recognition that technology flows often are more beneficial than capital flows; its government has intervened to assure negotiation of maximum benefits. Governments of technology-importing countries are typically concerned only with the fiscal and financial issues of a foreign investment or license agreement—tax rates, foreign exchange regulations governing remittance of profits or royalties, import and export conditions attached by either party—all aimed at maximizing the inflow of capital and limiting the outflow of earnings.[26] Little attention is paid to getting for the host country the most appropriate technology among alternative sources

25. National Academy of Sciences/Brazil National Research Council, *Industrial Research as a Factor in Economic Development*, Report of the Joint Study Group on Industrial Research (Washington: NAS, 1968).
26. Quinn, "Technology Transfer by Multinational Companies."

or to negotiating commitments by the investor or licensor regarding training, local research, assistance to local suppliers, customer-service programs, or future product development. Many countries would find it well worth the cost in expert manpower to establish this negotiation or review capacity in their investment-approval offices.

Natural Resource Surveys

A national industrial technology program also requires that the government inventory and discover mineral and water resources and project demand on them for energy and industrial uses. It should be equipped to suggest alternative sources and to assure current state-of-the-art knowledge on natural resource exploitation. Some of this information may be gathered in government ministries, some in independent resource-planning centers, some in a central industrial technology research institute. In any case, there should also be a natural resources unit in a central government economic development planning office.

National Industrial Research Institutes and Training Centers

It is only at about this point in a listing of priority measures that it becomes sensible to consider large investments in national industrial research centers. Without the prior steps, user demand for the output of public research and training institutions is likely to be weak and the signals guiding their efforts toward marketable industrial technology will be faint or faulty.

The rare success stories in public industrial research and advanced training have been based on market-oriented management, a national commitment to industrial progress, and actual demand for the ideas, graduates, and material products of the programs. Where national institutions have fallen into disuse or cloistered isolation, the symptoms of failure have included inadequate operating funds, preoccupation with academic science, unfocused programs, incomplete development of a potential industrial innovation, second-rate staffs imposed by civil service rules, and poor management. The fundamental malady, however, has been failure to build into these institutions an organizational and financial compulsion to serve market demand.

Much the same can be said of efforts to create a competence in industrial technology through university programs. Good students are not long attracted to science and technology programs when employment opportunities are stagnant or only slowly growing. Good and relevant training is almost inconceivable without the regular exposure of students to external activity in their fields and of professors to the stimulus of research and consultation on concrete problems of industry and government service agencies. Where demand for the output of research and development programs is rising, a small pool of skilled manpower can be inspired to higher performance and encouraged to undertake in-service training. The "brain drain" of scientists and technicians cannot be checked unless comprehensive steps are taken to create challenging opportunities for service at home.

Two Models for Public Institutes

Most countries attempting to invigorate their industrial technology programs face the problem of what to do with an accumulation of established national or provincial research organs. These are typically small, poorly equipped or financially starved sidelines of government agencies responsible for industry, natural resources, and materials standards and testing.

Their managements only rarely conceive of industrial research as part of an integrated production and marketing function. Consequently, their choice of research projects is haphazard and their capacity to carry an idea through to application very limited. If they could be made to work better, they would complement the governmental measures aimed at stimulating private creation and acquisition of industrial technology.

A Standard Model

Brazil faced the necessity of increasing the payoff from its various national and state industrial development institutions. A joint team of the Brazilian National Research Council and the U.S. National Academy of Sciences studied its system and designed a model to guide the reform process.[27] The team recommended that existing research establishments be reorganized, and in some cases consolidated, and that private research initiatives be subsidized by a special public fund to accomplish the objectives it outlined. If within two years these steps had not been taken, a new national institute of applied research should be established.

In either case, the model to be followed called for a private, nonprofit institution dedicated to public service. It should be organized to perform multidisciplinary research and to attack a broad range of problems faced by industry and government. It should develop a strong capability in management and techno-economic sciences as well as natural and engineering sciences and orient its work to broad economic and resource development studies. It should adopt a practical, user- or market-oriented attitude, continuously responsive to the needs of Brazil and of actual or potential clientele. Market demand and availabilities of staff and other resources should determine its service programs.

27. NAS, *Industrial Research as a Factor in Economic Development.*

The bulk of the institution's research, whether governmental or private, should be paid for by clients, but some funds could be available for the institute's own initiatives. To bring its services to the attention of potential clients and to make Brazilian industry and government aware of the benefits of applied research, the institute should conduct aggressive sales campaigns followed by periodic meetings, seminars, and workshops for clients and potential clients. It should exchange staff with universities, use professors and graduate students for part-time work, arrange for joint use of equipment and joint seminars and research projects, and offer part-time teaching assignments at the institute. Where feasible it should use subcontracting arrangements so as to minimize duplication of capital and staff and upgrade the other institutions.

The institution should be managed by a self-perpetuating board of directors, with no more than one-third of its members from interested government agencies. The board would be limited to electing a president, approving the annual budget and major fields of activity, and establishing general policies, without involvement in details. Staff salaries should be competitive with the best available in Brazilian industry to encourage mobility between institute and industrial employment. In-service training of staff should be continuously provided. A start-up operating fund (apart from anticipated fee income) of $5 million to $6 million, or an endowment of $10 million, should be contributed by industry, government, and foreign assistance agencies. The institute should have a contract affiliation with a leading foreign industrial research organization.

The Korean Model

Korea's Institute of Science and Technology promises to set an example of what can be accomplished when the national psychological and economic climate is favorable and the internal operating principles of a national research center are sound.

When the institute was conceived in 1965, Korea was launching an export-centered industrialization drive. Its success depended on continuous diversification of manufacturing and food processing, rising productivity, and design and quality levels competitive with Japan, Taiwan, Hong Kong, and other established industrial centers. Korea's industry was small, financially weak, and inexperienced in designing and producing for export. It could not generate its own technological innovations. Only a few Korean scientists or industrial employees were experienced in applied research. Other than an industrial testing laboratory and an atomic energy research center, there was no industrial research or advanced training center in applied technology. Many of Korea's trained natural scientists were remaining abroad after graduate education or emigrating to the better research opportunities abroad.

In short, there was strong social and market demand for a national industrial technology center, no prospect of Korean industry's private efforts satisfying much of this need, and some prospect of acquiring good staff through inducements to those overseas to return to an attractive institution. Other conditions for success were deliberately constructed. The U.S. and Korean governments pledged generous financial support in getting the institute started. Long-term support was limited to an endowment fund, set up by the Korean government, leaving a short-fall requiring rising fee income from contract research to support the institute's operations when it reached maturity. A strong-minded Korean scientist-administrator and a first-class U.S. consulting contractor ("sister institution") designed a charter and operating plan that provided for real professional autonomy under a self-perpetuating board of directors.

The institute's president promptly recruited 24 expatriate

Korean scientists from the United States, Japan, and Europe, a rare reversal of the brain drain. Excellent physical facilities, including housing, and industry-scale salaries were among the lures used. At least as important was the evident determination of the institute to become a major force in Korea's rapid development. By the end of 1970 it had nearly 350 professional staff members, 53 with PhD degrees.

The institute's program includes contract research for industry and government, self-generated research on matters demonstrably useful to industrial development, and collaboration with government economic development agencies on long-range planning studies. The institute has helped plan development of a machine tool industry, the electronics industry, marine resources, energy production, and science and technology education. Its projects have ranged from fundamental studies to pilot plant operations in food technology, materials sciences, electronics, and chemical, electrical, and mechanical engineering. Five of its own initiatives in the first two years led to licensed production of new products. Very high proportions of its contract research in the first two years of substantial operation were put into immediate use in industrial production, a striking contrast with the record of industrial research institutes in some other countries.

Aggressive salesmanship built up a major contract research program before all of the institute's equipment and staff were in place. Further growth of this business seems to confirm expectations that the Institute of Science and Technology will be able to live on its fee income and endowment after 1973. Its five-year projection to 1974 estimated a workload of eight hundred projects valued at about $14.5 million.

The institute's early successes led to plans for a complex of related research and higher educational centers at the same location. It will include a graduate training center, the Korean Advanced Institute of Sciences, and a quasi-governmental public policy research center, in addition to the existing Science and Technology Information Center.

Roles for U.S. Technical Assistance

The conceptual framework for national industrial technology programs implies potential roles for U.S. technical assistance. The general U.S. mission is to help establish institutions for better management of technological innovation tailored to local resources and market opportunities. Several clusters of public activities in developing countries could benefit from foreign technical assistance.

Governments need to reappraise their financial, fiscal, and trade policies affecting industrial incentives in order to raise productivity, expand economic activity and employment, and select or design appropriate technologies. Foreign assistance in such a review and in planning for change can best be offered through development finance agencies or composite teams of UN and banking agency experts. The U.S. technical assistance agency should defer to them.

Developing countries need to assess and improve their institutions, public and private, dealing with industrial technology. Foreign experts can be of great help in assessing these institutions' effectiveness, a step that logically follows the initiation of policy reforms. The U.S. National Academy of Sciences and National Academy of Engineering have the capacity to mobilize teams of government, university, and private industry experts for short-term collaboration with public and private counterparts in developing countries. If an assessment is to be realistic and productive, it should involve—and ideally should be initiated by—the economic ministry and development planning office of the developing country, not just the science and industry community. The U.S. technical assistance agency should make known its readiness to recruit help in designing a national industrial technology program.

Techno-economic staffs must be added to national development planning bodies and development banks. This amounts to much more than training and employing a few engineers, or adding technology sections to decision documents written by economists and bankers. What is required is the addition of new staff with academic and career training in the integration of economic/financial and technological considerations in analysis and the retraining of existing staff to understand technological issues. Specialists in the major technical fields of a country's development, including transport, communications, and housing as well as manufacturing, should be readily available to development banks and economic planning agencies. The United States can contribute training grants for individual staff members, faculty for local institutions of scientific and technical education, and temporary expatriate staff specialists for new techno-economic units. The latter should normally be recruited as employees of the host institution with salary supplements paid by the U.S. aid program.

Research and training activities should be instituted in industrial companies and associations in developing countries. The United States has by far the world's greatest body of experience and pool of potential short-term staff for helping to bring about this innovation. Indirect or direct government subsidies are essential but not sufficient to launch successful nongovernmental research and training programs in most developing countries. A critical factor is qualified manpower to organize these programs in a market-oriented pattern and to staff some of the key positions in the initial period of operation, while local capabilities and experience are being built up. Retired or restless U.S. industrial research directors, in-service training directors, process and product design technicians, materials-handling and maintenance systems designers, and other specialists could—if carefully selected—fill this temporary need. Such expatriate staff members, employed by a company or industrial association (with salary supplements provided by the United States) for periods of three months to a year, would train local replacements or cohorts while acting on assigned jobs. The experience of the U.S. International Executive Service Corps (IESC) in recruiting short-term technical aid for general industrial management indicates that a private group would be likely to meet this need far better than the U.S. technical assistance agency's direct staff. The agency should consider sponsoring and partially financing such a program by a private intermediary.

Local public and private technical service and techno-economic consulting companies should be expanded. Many of the services required in economies short of managerial and technical skills are of the "nuts and bolts" variety. They cannot be supplied by high-priced alien firms, and they must be attuned to local customs and resources. The first step in strengthening local competence is to increase market demand for it, by attaching conditions to capital loans requiring borrowers to use these services and favoring local and joint-venture suppliers. Public subsidies, provided by the local government or foreign aid agencies through a local intermediary such as a productivity center, may be required to help small firms train their expanding staffs. The U.S. technical assistance program should stand ready to provide temporary expatriate staff members to these enterprises, again working through a private intermediary. The principal manpower sources would be retired members of U.S. economic and engineering consulting firms with experience in developing countries. Placement would have to be made with due regard to potential or apparent conflicts of interest with the employee's former firm.

Effective natural resource survey and planning capacities must be built. One of the more successful U.S. technical assistance activities has been the long-term professional collaboration of natural resource agencies in the developing countries and such U.S. government agencies as the Geological Survey, Bureau of Mines, and Forest Service. Some aid program "graduates" have continued these arrangements at their own expense. In future collaborative work, U.S. program managers should encourage greater attention to research on specific technologies utilizing industrial raw materials more efficiently. Assistance should include participation by U.S. experts in local and regional research projects, provision of laboratory equipment, training, and partial staffing of urgent reconnaissance surveys.

Not until it is clear that the climate and institutional network for technological innovation in the requesting country are being systematically improved should U.S. assistance for public research centers be considered. Only then is the necessarily large-scale and long-term U.S. financial and technical assistance likely to be a reasonably good risk. Even so, firm commitments on both sides should be withheld during a period of thorough reconnaissance and project planning by the U.S. professional contractor and the host institution. The main fields of research and development activity should be determined before the final agreement for technical and financial support is made.

In some countries it may be sensible to have several specialized institutes serving various growth industries; in others, consolidation of services in a single institute with specialized divisions will be more efficient. Where little or no local capacity to provide simple technical services to industry exists, planning must resolve whether the research institute or a separate technical service agency should undertake this work.

Particular attention should be given to whether research on transportation and construction is being adequately provided. Typically, these areas have been slighted in science-oriented research centers established in the developing countries over the past ten to fifteen years.

The marketing and sales policies and methods of the industrial research institute, which largely determine its practicality and solvency, should be a main concern of U.S. technical assistance. The United States might make a highly productive investment by supplementing sales and marketing staffs with short-term specialists (recruited by the U.S. professional contractor, or "sister institution," or by a specialized agency like the IESC) in the early years of a project.

Support of individual projects at existing industrial technology centers will often be a better investment than starting a wholly new center. This amounts to selective expansion and channeling of the work of national centers. It usually will involve provision of financial support for the project budget, equipment, and specialized U.S. staff by the U.S. technical assistance agency. If the research centers of several countries are participating in the investigation of a single problem, a lead institution should be designated or some other arrangement should be made to assure comparability of the research results and division of labor. The project plan should provide for a prior determination of industrial customer interest in the expected results, feasible participation by local enterprises in the research and design work, and arrangements for other follow-on activity in and with local enterprises.

Multilateral Approaches

Almost every international meeting on industrial or natural resource development over the past decade has proposed multilateral machinery to close the technology gap. Suggestions have included a "world bank for technology," a "patents bank for developing countries," regional or international "technology transfer centers" or institutes, technical information clear-inghouses, and international agreements providing for technology price discounts for less developed countries or "most favored nation" terms of trade in technologies.

The rationale common to these schemes is the need for the international community to intervene collectively to offset the poor countries' disadvantages in either the creation of or the bargaining for industrial technology. Much of the discussion of the "world plan of action" prepared by the UN Advisory Committee on the Application of Science and Technology to Development dealt with the mechanisms and feasibility of new plans for international action proposed by UNIDO and the UN Conference on Trade and Development.

Several stubborn obstacles to multilateral action in this complex field often are taken too lightly. First, if technology transfer is to result in efficient production, it must involve a great deal more than simply handing over drawings, specifications, and instructions. There must be sustained relationships between a thoroughly knowledgeable supplier of the technology and the buyer or user of it. The user must undertake adaptations, engineering, layout of production facilities, marketing, and other innovations and training, often with the help of those experienced in the applications of the particular technology. Second, owners of the most valuable industrial technology are unlikely to give away the proprietary rights that resulted from costly research efforts. Third, even if liberal terms for the publication and release of technological knowledge and designs were arranged through collective action, most of the developing countries would have great difficulty applying them without extensive investments in human skills. International action cannot obviate primary reliance upon commercial channels and the need for systematic action at the national and enterprise levels.

Within these limitations, there are promising opportunities

for regional or even global cooperation in training and research or advisory work on both natural resource and industrial technology problems. For example, regional UN commissions or technological training centers might establish panels of experts in special fields of water, mineral, or energy studies from which governments of developing countries could draw teams for sector or preliminary feasibility studies. The international composition of these teams would be an advantage in politically sensitive fields.

Regional organizations also might identify a few industrial technology research needs that by their nature require a multicountry, comparative effort. They could arrange for a leading institution in the region or in a developed country to coordinate the participation of research centers and enterprises in the project. Among the subjects that might be treated in multisite research are methods of economically extracting and refining low-grade mineral ores; labor-intensive means of using readily available soils and fibers in the fabrication of cheap building materials; and means of using ferro-concrete or plastics in the manufacture of boats, barges, pipes, storage bins, and other mass-use items.

Multilateral agencies will normally be the most acceptable sources of assistance in strengthening the capabilities of developing countries to bargain more shrewdly with private foreign owners of industrial technology. Many spin-off benefits of licensing arrangements and foreign investment are being overlooked by enterprises and governments in these countries as they weigh the financial or fiscal, but not the technological, advantages of equipment, processes, and training offered commercially. Small companies, particularly, need the advice or negotiating assistance of a knowledgeable public official or local consulting firm on these questions. Training in this specialized field should be a useful role for multilateral banks, UNIDO, or regional economic institutions.

Summary

Neither agriculture nor industry nor the services can independently accelerate the pace at which wealth and employment opportunities are created over a long period in most countries. The right concentration of effort and measures in each sector can only be judged in light of each country's circumstances and opportunities. In almost any case, however, mounting social demands will call for more vigorous exploitation of industry's potential both directly to open new fields of economic activity and employment and indirectly to stimulate faster growth in agricultural and service jobs and income.

This is no mean feat. It requires governments of developing countries to make complex and sometimes politically hazardous changes in policies or institutions that influence industrial growth. A coherent strategy must deal with trade, savings, investment, training, technology, and a host of other supporting forces. For many countries, success will hinge on support from the industrialized nations, international agencies, and international enterprises provided through trade opportunities and crucial increments of capital and technology. The United States in its public and private roles can either frustrate or materially assist these countries' industrial development, on which much else depends.

A positive response by the United States should include—but by no means be limited to—technical assistance focused on an aspect of the industrial development process in which it has outstanding competence and the less developed countries have critical limitations. This is, broadly, the market-oriented creation and application of technology. The main thrust of U.S. or multilateral technical assistance in this field should be on improving indigenous capabilities, both in private enterprise and in public institutions, to acquire, adapt, and use industrial and natural resource technologies. The feasibility of the suggested training, research, institution-building, commerce, and investment necessary to this depends on parallel action by both developing countries and the international community to change the policies and attitudes that determine whether and how opportunities for technological advance will be exploited.

There should be no illusion that the technical approaches suggested here will alone provide the missing ingredient sparking a surge of socially rational industrial growth in severely handicapped countries. But in concert with other essential actions this unique American contribution may help to reduce some critical industrial handicaps.

CHAPTER FOUR

Health: Prescriptions
for Reform

GOOD HEALTH expresses or implies most of the goals of development. To a degree difficult to measure, it is a precondition of the accelerated economic progress that, in turn, is essential to broadly shared health progress. Good health for whom and by what means are becoming political questions of growing urgency in most countries, rich as well as poor.

If better health for all is the objective, poor countries confront a set of problems for which Western experience offers few applicable solutions. The case for fresh, original approaches through research and experimental programs in health care is at least as clear as in agricultural development. If means are found for reducing the health handicaps of the poor majority in Latin America, Asia, and Africa, they may also answer some of the problems of the lower income minority in the United States.

The challenge of work that clamors to be done and of ways to go about doing it must be considered in the perspective of what has been accomplished. The dramatic achievements include a decline in overall or crude death rates that began in most of the less developed countries early in the twentieth century and accelerated during the last two decades. (Death rates remain nearly twice as high, again overall, as in the most developed countries—many times higher among infants and

86

young children.) Colonial administrations in many cases improved distribution of food, reduced tribal and religious conflicts, and extended preventive health services to some of the population. In the period of independence and international assistance since World War II, major famines have been curbed, and curative and preventive medicine has warded off massive attacks by a few of the great killers of the past. Preventive campaigns against malaria, yellow fever, and other vector-borne diseases have improved worker efficiency in some tropical countries. For the elite, largely in cities, who could afford Western-style medical care coupled with better diets and home sanitation, modernization has brought both relief from disease and longer lives.

One of the paradoxes of this age is that great success in reducing infant mortality and prolonging life in the less developed countries has intensified their problems of health care and general development. Birthrates geared to high mortality expectations have not declined with the death rates. Capital formation, job creation, and social services have not been able to keep pace with the rapid growth of population concentrated in the nonproductive age groups. More people are surviving, but they are ill fed and ill housed and therefore vulnerable to debilitating disease. The opportunity gaps between the fortunate, healthy few and the chronically disease-burdened majority remain.

A superficial reading of history suggests that medical technology has been primarily responsible for achieving the reduction in mortality and that it should in the future be equally—and independently—successful in reducing morbidity. This is probably an illusion. The relatively recent introduction of modern "wonder drugs," the mass campaigns against four of the major tropical diseases (malaria, yellow fever, smallpox, and yaws), and the surge in medical school output by the developing countries seem to have only slightly accelerated the

downward curve in death rates. All these modernizations plus
the advent of publicly financed health clinics in rural areas undoubtedly have helped to lower death rates and raise economic
productivity. Studies of Western countries, however, suggest
that the larger influences on death rates are rising general income levels, education, food availability, improved environmental sanitation, and water supply.[1] This seems likely to be
the pattern also in the developing countries, only a small fraction of whose total populations has regularly been reached by
curative or preventive medical services.

Continued progress in lowering death rates and particularly
in reducing the burden of disease in the low-income countries
is likely to depend on the effectiveness of comprehensive economic and social development programs, including widespread
application of both preventive and curative medicine and nutritional improvement. A comprehensive approach is demanded by the nature of the major illnesses of the poor countries: diarrheal diseases, particularly in small children, worm
infestation in all age groups, schistosomiasis and other parasitic
diseases peculiar to different regions, tuberculosis, trachoma,
leprosy, all continually reappearing and spreading out of environments of filth, ignorance of hygiene, and poor nutrition.
In the villages and swelling city slums where most people live,
infectious disease flourishes in alternating mud and dust, human and animal excrement, insects, rats, and contaminated
food and water.

Children suffer most severely. Those under age five make up
about 15 percent of the total population of the less developed

1. Philip Hauser, "Population Growth Patterns in an Unstable
World," *U.S. Air Force Medical Service Digest*, Vol. 20 (January 1969),
p. 14; Walsh McDermott, "Modern Medicine and the Demographic Disease Pattern of Overly Traditional Societies: A Technologic Misfit," in
Manpower for the World's Health (Washington: Association of American Medical Colleges, 1966), p. 142.

countries but suffer nearly one-half of the recorded deaths, compared with 7 percent among this age group in the United States. About 30 million of the annual deaths in the less developed countries are among children under five, and about half of these children die of intestinal infections compounded by poor nutrition.[2]

Children with respiratory and diarrheal diseases are largely beyond the reach of the advanced technology of clinical medicine. "If children sick with these diseases do reach the physician, there are sharp limits to what he can do. Diarrhea and pneumonia are often not affected by antibiotics, and the frequent presence of malnutrition makes even supportive therapy difficult or futile. And even these interventions by the physician, whether or not they are therapeutically effective, are only sporadic ripples in the running tide of disease."[3] These children's lives are saturated with the causes of disease, unrecognized or accepted with resignation.

Mortality is the measurable tip of the iceberg. More difficult to measure is the burden of morbidity and related nutritional debility among the economically active age groups. Fragmentary reporting of disease incidence in most of the less developed countries, supplemented by detailed samplings in a few countries or districts, has permitted only rough estimation of the disease and nutritional problems of specific population groups. All authorities agree, however, that disease-induced interruption of work, lassitude, and lowered learning ability apply a staggering drag on economic productivity and dynamism.

Economic development and effective health programs have lowered mortality rates, but birthrates have not declined as rapidly. Parents accustomed to high mortality among their

2. Estimate by Office of Health, Agency for International Development (AID), 1970.

3. John Bryant, *Health and the Developing World* (Cornell University Press, 1969), p. 39.

children continue to have large families, intensifying population pressures on limited resources and putting brakes on progress—including health improvement. Effective health-protection programs accompanied by effective birth-control programs can make a positive contribution to economic and social development. Disease-reduction programs can ultimately shift parental motivations toward smaller families, although in the short run they are likely to aggravate the population problem.

The interdependence of health and development is apparent in this cursory description. Morbidity saps productivity, limiting the resources available for improved nutrition, education, sanitation, and preventive and curative medicine. Thus the restraints on progress imposed by disease are prolonged. If, on the other hand, all available resources are concentrated on the single variable, health services, the result might be prolonged economic stagnation and ultimately collapse of the expanded health services. Obviously, these broad generalizations may not be true or important in some settings. They do, however, suggest the dilemmas that confound those who design development strategy.

Of course, health is more than an economic development factor. It is a basic human value in all societies. Its proper share of national income investment in the developing countries is a political decision that cannot be determined solely—or today even accurately—by cost-benefit calculations. Waiting for economic development to create the conditions for improved general health, without attempting to make better use of existing resources for direct attacks on the great health handicaps, is likely to be bad economic policy as well as bad politics.

Health Programs in the Developing Countries

Health care systems in the developing countries, like those in the West, have grown out of tradition, market responses, political gestures and promises, foreign advice or example, and —occasionally—comprehensive planning. If their objectives were solely to provide curative medical service to those in the larger population centers who could afford it or who had access to subsidized hospitals and clinics, they would get good marks for steady progress. If, as political policies typically declare, their objective is to raise health standards for all, a few systems would get a passing grade for effort but most would be judged a failure on universal coverage.

In the past fifteen years the developing countries have established or expanded more than two hundred and fifty medical schools, sent thousands of their educated elite abroad for medical training, and added courses or departments of preventive and, in a few cases, community medicine to their training programs. The vast majority of their doctors congregate in the cities, seeking private practice or at best working only part-time in public hospitals and clinics. So many stay abroad after graduation from medical school or emigrate later—an inevitable response to enormous income differentials—that they have become a major source of medical manpower in the United States and some Western European countries. One-third of the interns and residents in U.S. hospitals in 1969 were foreign trained, and about three-fourths of these came from less developed countries.[4] In this brain drain the United States is literally reaping a human profit on aid to medical education in and for the developing countries.

In the less developed countries an average of less than one full-fledged doctor and one nurse is available to serve 50,000 persons in rural areas; in some extremely poor or remote areas the ratios are closer to one to 1 million residents. These countries typically spend about $2 per capita in public funds and somewhat more in private funds for all types of health services,

4. Carl Taylor, "International Health: Getting More Than We Give," *Roche Medical Image and Commentary*, Vol. 12, No. 4 (April 1970).

in environments where disease is far more prevalent than in
the West. (The U.S. figure of about $250 per capita for health
care is not comparable in many respects, but it suggests something of the financial pinch on health planning in the low-
income countries.)

That $2 per capita average public outlay—less than 50 cents
in some African and Asian countries and $20 or more in some
Latin American countries—must cover environmental sanitation programs in villages, towns, and city slums; public health
immunization and other preventive medicine; free or partially
subsidized central, district, and village health centers or clinics;
hospital subsidies; training of auxiliary and paramedical personnel; health research; and administrative costs. In some
countries the national health budget also bears the costs of
nutrition programs and part of the costs of medical education
and health guidance in schools and information media.

At these levels of funding, what is presented to the people
as a health system is likely to be a fraud. A patient walks or
rides great distances to reach a clinic where he waits hours for
a physician or auxiliary who has neither the time nor the facilities to make a careful diagnosis. Then a word of advice, a bot-
tle of medicine, and a slow walk back to the same home environment. When the problem recurs, the patient may not
bother to go through that again. The clinic's physician may be
available only for a few hours a day or week, squeezed into his
private practice. The assistant medical officer manning a clinic
may be under directions that circumscribe what he can do to
help a patient in the absence of a physician. The sick peasant
or slum dweller may shun the clinic because he senses disdain
or a racial or class barrier in the manner of the professional
staff of the clinic. The clinic may nevertheless be crowded with
patients whose ailments would not need medical examination
if they knew some simple personal hygiene; at the same time,
others may be dying without ever seeing a doctor.

Preventive medicine services also may be more impressive on paper than in reality. Sanitation services that boast all the standard staff units and programs may have thin and spotty coverage, stereotyped methods, and, above all, budgets that are barely a drop in the bucket of filth and customs. Immunization and insect-control campaigns have made great contributions against a few diseases, often under international assistance programs, but these are hampered by administrative problems, failure of all the residents of an area to cooperate, or biological resistance to the drugs and insecticides employed.

Money is the basic limitation. Low budgets and salaries limit the extent and quality of services, the willingness of professionally trained people to serve and make a commitment to public service programs, and the depth of research directed at finding better ways of meeting needs. Most of the money must come from public budgets if the masses of the population are to be protected. If public health budgets rise no faster than per capita national income rises, the $2 per capita governmental outlay for health services is not likely to reach the grand sum of $4 until 1990 or later.

In short, financial reality demands that the developing countries find ways of making their health services much more efficient than in the past. They cannot afford to copy the West's very costly and inefficient methods of distributing health care. Even if they could tolerate the human suffering, their economic development interests demand that they reduce the waste of productive energy exacted by trying to do a little of everything poorly.

If they want better health for the majority of their people, they will have to make truly revolutionary changes—in the health (and nutrition) knowledge and habits of their peoples, in the functional analysis and redesign of their health delivery systems, in the quality of their preventive and environmental programs, in the orientation and motivation of their medical schools and medical professions, in the training and utilization of paramedical and auxiliary personnel, and in the financing of the whole health sector, public and private.

They will need external help, including that of other countries in the same boat, in the form of fresh ideas and analytical skills, more relevant training and research, more urgent development of applicable biological and managerial technologies, and money.

The Key Problems

Revitalization of U.S. and multilateral programs of technical assistance depends on an orderly conception of which among the awesome array of health problems are critical and which of these can be profitably attacked. Some of course are exclusively problems of population or nutrition. Following are some key problems that can be dealt with through health research and technical assistance:[5]

1. Pollution of soil and water with human wastes; both financially and technically, extension of present methods of water supply and waste disposal is unpromising.

2. High mortality and morbidity among infants and children, largely due to complexes of enteric and respiratory infections and malnutrition; this is believed to deter the practice of fertility control in some societies.

3. Widespread ignorance of the causes of disease; health programs consequently are frustrated, public health clinics are overloaded, and major engineering or other development projects that exacerbate disease threats are sometimes undertaken.

4. Wasteful use of scarce resources in the treatment of pre-

5. Adapted from Lee Howard and others, "Key Problems in Health" (staff paper, AID, 1970; processed).

ventable illnesses, where less expensive preventive measures are known but not applied.

5. Waste of food energy; widespread infections and fevers increase body metabolism, accelerating the use of calories or proteins causing nutritional imbalance, that is, secondary malnutrition.

6. Denial of continuous access to arable areas; land cannot be used because of the threat of such vector-borne diseases as malaria, onchocerciasis, and trypanosomiasis (the latter precludes cattle raising in much of Africa).

7. Lack of health analysis and planning competence in most governments and the relatively low status of this function in nearly all development planning bodies and assistance agencies.

8. Token approaches to the delivery of national health services; most programs reach or attract only a little over 10 percent of the target populations, placing severe constraints on programs to control population growth and to improve nutrition.

9. Geographical misallocation and functional misuse of trained health manpower; disproportionate emphasis in training and practice is placed on private curative services to the neglect of preventive and rural service; many countries fail to exploit the potential of auxiliary and paramedical manpower, while the brain drain siphons off professional manpower.

10. Values and attitudes that resist change or perpetuate inefficiency, corruption, and poor rapport between people and government program staffs.

The World Health Organization, in the 1969 annual report of its director-general, combined several of these items in a single issue of unsound "health infrastructure" in the developing countries. Some doctors would put the medical profession itself at the top of the problem list.

An analysis of key problems, within a particular country or

region, can reveal the areas where health programs should be reformed and where technical assistance might be concentrated. A health sector analysis is, itself, a fruitful field for international professional collaboration or aid. Through it, the health and general development authorities of a country may reach a better understanding of their interdependence and appreciate the need for reconciling or defining national program priorities in specific terms. It gives the developing country an opportunity to size up the usefulness of foreign experts and their fresh viewpoints without entering a long-term obligation. If carried out with candor and objectivity, the exercise reveals gaps between program words and actual performance and spotlights areas that require more detailed study, technological research, and field experiments.

A comprehensive health sector analysis takes time and talent. Aid agencies have not pressed for such studies or offered to provide quickly the competent supplemental or advisory staffs needed by most developing countries to undertake them. Such studies may seem to a health minister to threaten only more studies and greater risk of public or political embarrassment. They are, therefore, rarely initiated in developing countries. What passes for systematic planning usually is a mixture of forward projections of existing programs, detailed examination of a few discrete elements of the national health system, and periodic adjustments to emergencies. In a few countries, more complete reappraisals are undertaken for five-year development plans, but these tend to become annexes designed largely to state the "consumption" claims of health programs on the national budget.

Health Research Priorities

Some of the present knowledge of tropical health problems is based on work begun in the colonial era. Many of the medical education and research facilities in developing countries were established then. During World War II the United States intensified its tropical health study in order to protect U.S. troops operating in the Pacific, Southern Asia, and the Panama Canal Zone and Caribbean theater. As the colonial and wartime motivations declined, so did budgets, staff, and training in these fields. Neither private foundations and charities, which had long been active in special fields of preventive medicine and hospital development, nor the international and national aid agencies picked up the slack in tropical health research.

Apart from intensive work on malaria and several diseases of domesticated animals of the subtropics, research on the great diseases afflicting the less developed regions has been fragmentary, leisurely, underfunded, and increasingly understaffed. This has been true in the extreme of the operational and community health fields.

Researchers, like most people with rare skills, go where money beckons or professional recognition and prizes are to be won. Even in the developing countries, the incentives for medical researchers have been stacked in favor of work on subjects currently in vogue in the West, such as fundamental molecular and genetic studies. The World Health Organization (WHO) has tried to enlarge or sustain interest and competence in medical research relevant to the developing countries, but its small budget for research and its policy of broadly distributing token grants have precluded concentrated attack on key problems. Its fragmented approach to health research is not atypical; U.S. and European programs show the same pattern.

At the end of 1968, WHO had grants outstanding on 711 active research projects in 430 institutions in 77 countries. Seventy-five percent of its research contracts recently have been for less than $2,000, and most of the rest were also very small. Only 1.7 percent of the projects were in public health services. While 41 percent were in communicable disease research, the field is large and the work of hundreds of participating institutions could hardly be coordinated beyond an exchange of information and establishment of some standards in the review process for grants.

Somewhat similarly, the Pan American Health Organization (PAHO) lists 104 active research projects in a program determined primarily by the coincidence of interests of grant applicants and donors to PAHO's research fund. It does concentrate the bulk of its grants in three strong regional research institutions—the Pan American Zoonoses Center, the Pan American Foot and Mouth Disease Center, and the Institution of Nutrition of Central America and Panama—plus its own staff and a few national institutions.

The landmark study *Tropical Health*, issued in 1962 by the U.S. National Academy of Sciences/National Research Council, described U.S. research grants in tropical health as isolated bits of activity supported by the armed forces, the National Institutes of Health, and the private foundations. It found little relationship between major health needs of the tropical countries and the research grant subjects. It advocated "broader planning of certain types of basic research together with follow-up through developmental stages, so that basic research results may be more quickly and advantageously applied to the solution of public health problems in the tropics."[6]

Most of the biological research tasks highlighted by *Tropical Health* ten years ago and by the WHO in the mid-1960s have stubbornly persisted. These include better means of prevention and treatment of bacillary dysentery and leprosy; a faster-acting treatment for trachoma and better knowledge of its

6. National Academy of Sciences/National Research Council, Division of Medical Sciences, *Tropical Health, A Report on a Study of Health Needs and Resources* (Washington: NAS/NRC, 1962), p. 295.

viral agents; a multifunctional antimalaria drug; control and chemotherapy tools for fighting schistosomiasis; an effective anticholera immunization; a long-acting, low-cost defense against spirochaetal diseases without allergic hazards; and better understanding of the relationships of nutrition and infectious diseases.

Much of the progress that has been made possible by research in the last decade on vector-borne diseases now is being threatened by increasing biological resistance to the chemicals currently employed. Human resistance to established drugs is setting back progress in treating trypanosomiasis in Africa; no effective drug seems to have been found for its Latin American form, Chagas' disease.

These are not grounds for despair. They are reminders that health research is a virtually endless process and that the quality and intensity of effort applied to the health problems of the tropics have been very inadequate.

Funds, skilled and dedicated researchers, and facilities for undertaking research and testing results are likely to remain severely limited. These precious assets must be applied to the most important needs of the greatest number, not dissipated on minor activities designed to satisfy the personal interests of individual scientists or on disconnected bits of effort. Again, as in agricultural research, the clear imperative is to create a system of research management that links basic, applied, and operational studies in an efficient continuum.

Determination of health priorities must proceed from an understanding of the interrelationships of particular health investments and economic and social development. Health policy and planning studies are both a function of health research and a prerequisite to setting national health research priorities.

Over the coming decade, health research priorities of the less developed countries will vary considerably by country and region. They will largely fall into clusters of needs in the operation of health services, the mobilization of manpower, and the design of basic and applied tools for solving biomedical problems.

Those in the operation of health services include: functional analysis of the jobs to be done and means of reallocating many tasks now performed by doctors to less broadly trained auxiliaries, technicians, clerks, and machines; comprehensive analysis in pilot operations of alternative means of delivering health services; controlled testing of alternative means of mass hygiene education; determination of marginal costs of specific preventive and curative health services at different degrees of geographic and substantive coverage; and investigation of means of financing health care by such supplements to budgetary allocations as insurance, service fees, lotteries, foreign assistance, and deferred reimbursement of tuition subsidies by doctors.

Problems in the mobilization of health manpower that should be investigated include the measurement of professional, auxiliary, and technical training goals, curricula, and output against the essential needs of a country's health services; use of educational technologies to improve training, especially of auxiliary and paramedical personnel; means of increasing the productivity of existing staff and mobilizing manpower outside the health field to serve the needs of the health program; experimental approaches to motivating or inducing health workers to serve the whole community, especially the remote and poorer elements; methods of educating doctors in social sciences and public administration with minimum sacrifice of medical training or deferral of medical service; and means of educating and motivating mothers, who are likely to be the providers of 90 percent of what passes for health care.

The basic and applied biomedical tools that should be developed through research include field and supporting laboratory studies of the synergism of malnutrition and enteric infections;

means of strengthening immunity and simple, decisive chemotherapy against bacillary diarrhea in children; more effective
chemical and genetic methods of controlling the vectors of
major diseases: malaria, schistosomiasis, onchocerciasis, trypanosomiasis, Chagas' disease, and filariasis; improved drugs
for treatment of these major diseases plus cholera, tuberculosis, leprosy, and venereal diseases; and effective and practicable
immunization against cholera.

The research objective in all these cases is not simply to produce an acceptable curative or preventive technology. It
should also be to find the most effective means of coping with
the epidemiologic aspects of the disease so as to determine
what changes in individual living habits, environmental conditions, and community health practices will best combat the
disease.

Research Management

The general objectives of health research are, in order of
priority, to learn to use existing biomedical knowledge and
technical resources more efficiently, in both training and service operations; to improve the preventive and curative procedures and products within the limits of existing knowledge;
and to expand the fundamental knowledge to make possible
new and more efficient health applications. International development agencies should follow this order of priority in their
financial support of health research. Traditionally, health research has given very little systematic attention to efficiency of
operations, for it was a matter of little interest to scientists,
medical schools, and research program directors. The evolution of preventive and community medicine as respectable
fields of scholarship has only slightly altered this neglect. The
plight of the poor countries now argues strongly for a sharp

reorientation of health research toward operations and preventive medicine in field applications.

It does not follow, however, that the three-legged stool of health research should be made to stand on one leg, or that administrators should force all health research into their service. What is needed is better, not worse, balance. Good research management should obtain better balance in the composition of research programs, the disciplines engaged in health research, and the division of labor among institutions engaged in health research—all pointed at the urgent needs of the poor countries.

Operators and educators need a research orientation, and researchers and teachers an operations orientation. Systems analysts, economists, sociologists, and other nonmedical specialists should be engaged in health research, not just in studies of health delivery problems but also in application of drug and pesticide technology. Organized, comprehensive research teams should be directed toward clearly defined targets and have the financial and institutional support required to find all the answers from basic science and anthropology through test application of products.

If health research is to be reformed in these directions, more of it must shift to the scenes of application—the developing countries' research centers, universities, and communities. This is necessary if research is to be related to local conditions, extended smoothly into field experiments, and fed back into training programs. This deliberate shift of the research locus to the developing countries can eventually strengthen their problem-solving competence generally and spur educational modernization.

The immediate prospects for instituting these suggested reforms in research management for the developing countries are dim. The United States, particularly, has very limited experience and little readily available expertise for health operational research. Few institutions have interdisciplinary teams (or the facility for assembling them) versed in the nonmedical aspects of community health operations in an Asian, African, or Latin American setting. Much of the world's technological capacity is in the United States and other developed countries, where personal incentives tend to hold scientists to their home bases. Research funding in the rich countries will always be directed more toward domestic interests than to the needs of foreign communities. Research stands far down the ranks of claimants on the budgets of the health ministries and medical schools in the less developed countries.

All these constraints can and will be eased, unevenly and over many years. Operational research talent must be developed, ways must be found to shift the weight of incentives working on at least some technological research institutions and individuals, applicable findings of Western medical and related scientific research must be quickly tapped, and health and financial authorities of the developing countries must be persuaded of the value of applied and operational research. For the nearer term, only marginal reductions of the limitations on research capacity can be anticipated.

A number of existing and proposed health research institutions suggest what realistically can be done. For instance, the Institute of Nutrition of Central America and Panama (INCAP) is located at the center of its service area; combined with that advantage is its access to the best laboratory-based talent in the United States and Latin American countries. Contracts with U.S. universities and with private food industry firms operating in Latin America give it resources many times greater than a regional laboratory could assemble and support. It is linked with the University of San Carlos, Guatemala, and with the Massachusetts Institute of Technology for advanced training and with extension services of the Central American countries for field testing. Its professional leadership gives strong direction to all its research, gets results, and thereby assures continuing financial support. It concentrates on the most important health problem of Central America. Its recent studies on the interrelationships of malnutrition and childhood enteric infections illustrate the institute's capacity to contribute to a worldwide network of research on this top-priority problem.

The Pakistan-SEATO (Southeast Asia Treaty Organization) Cholera Research Laboratory has teamed local and U.S. scientists in field research and advisory services in Southeast Asia; meanwhile, home-based specialists in a dozen U.S. public and private laboratories are attempting to develop a better cholera vaccine. The staff of the center in Dacca treats cholera cases, devises and teaches improved cholera therapies, and conducts vaccine field trials. These operational efforts provide practical guidance for laboratory research. The U.S. National Institutes of Health and AID have provided major support for the program, and the National Communicable Disease Center in Atlanta, Georgia, has collaborated on its epidemiologic studies.

The operating principles of this laboratory and the Institute of Nutrition are to concentrate on a single major problem, pursue solutions from basic research through field application, put direction of the whole research effort under a single manager, and disperse the research components among public and private organizations most competent to do it at their normal operating bases.

These principles were adopted in a plan for intensive attack on four major parasitic diseases outlined by the WHO. A center to direct comprehensive research on causes, prevention, and treatment would be established for each of the diseases—schistosomiasis, trypanosomiasis, onchocerciasis, and filariasis. WHO would organize each center in cooperation with a host institution in a tropical country that combined a high incidence of one of the diseases and some other advantages for research center operation. The host institution would provide space and some laboratory and field staff. The WHO would provide equipment and supplies and supervise the expert staff of individual scientists or outstanding research institutions that would undertake at their home benches most of the laboratory studies. The system would take full advantage of continuing work elsewhere—such as AID-financed research on the tsetse fly and Rockefeller-supported studies on schistosomiasis snail control—through meetings, publications, and exchange of staff.

Strong bases for comprehensive research on other diseases are available for similar international collaborative programs. These include the East African Virus Research Institute and the Pan American Zoonoses Center. A prime candidate for a large-scale program of coordinated international research, probably involving several field subcenters, is the prevention and treatment of bacillary dysentery in children. The program should be able to engage talent and attract national research funds and facilities not normally available for "foreign aid."

Regional tropical medicine research centers are less promising and global centers positively wrong approaches to the international health research needs. Such schemes would congregate the whole range of specialized talent and facilities required to deal with all or most of the diseases of a region or the globe in a single location or in several locations under single or committee supervision. This idea arises periodically in intergovernmental meetings. It has all the disadvantages of cost and recruitment problems that health research presents for any developing country. And it departs fatally from the sharp focus that is essential to effective management and completed solution of any single problem.

Operations research on health planning, delivery systems, and manpower has produced two outstanding models. One is a complex of planning, comprehensive social development, and community health experiments in and near Cali, Colombia. The other is a set of field studies in India, Turkey, and Iran by Johns Hopkins University's School of Public Health and testing of experimental community health designs in Narangwal, Punjab. The latter has demonstrated the feasibility of relying on specially trained auxiliary nurse–midwives in villages to provide preventive and curative services and family planning assistance under the once-weekly supervision of a visiting doctor and trained nurse. About 90 percent of the curative cases are handled by the nurse–midwife without further referral.

The Colombian operations research has three distinct components. A rural community health experiment in the very poor county of Candelaria features a simplified system of health care and family planning services, extensive use of trained volunteers, and various forms of preventive health education, all within the modest budget and manpower allocations of the Colombian public health system—one doctor, one nurse, and a handful of auxiliaries for a single county. In two years the project produced carefully measured statistical evidence of improved nutrition, a great reduction in diarrheal diseases, and falling (but still very high) birth rates, plus visual evidence of community improvement in other fields. The Pan American Federation of Associations of Medical Schools selected Candelaria as a center for international research and a model for replication in other parts of Latin America.

Urban health service reform in the context of broader urban development is being studied in low-income districts of the city of Cali by a multidisciplinary team staffed by the University of Valle, the state and city governments, and the Rockefeller Foundation. The newest Colombian experimental project is designed to find better ways of carrying out comprehensive health analysis, planning, and decision making in the whole range of social development affecting health. Its subject is the entire Cauca Valley of more than 2 million inhabitants. The WHO, PAHO, three U.S. universities, and two foundations have expressed interest in this project as a training ground and research center in community health planning.

None of these models is primarily designed to build health research competence in medical schools of the less developed countries. But in their operational research they engage the competence of medical schools or universities when and where they are the best source of available skills.

The objectives of developing research institutions and of producing research solutions converge naturally and efficiently in operations research. An objective, unfettered analysis of a health ministry's operational programs is usually impossible to get from the ministry's own staff, working alone. A joint, inter-disciplinary research team of ministry staff, university or medical school staff, and qualified foreign staff promises more useful results. Participation by faculty members and students in field operations research also serves the supremely important goal of making the medical school relevant to community needs. Participation by U.S. and other foreign scholars in the fields of community health and preventive medical administration can be arranged more comfortably for both sides if a local university or medical school has a large role in the research.

The already high costs of medical school operation and the paramount need to build community medicine doctrine and practice into medical curricula make it difficult to justify financing substantial biomedical research by medical schools in most developing countries. Yet they may offer the only promising nuclei of national health research competence. As a rule of thumb (with latitude for exceptions), research budgetary priority in developing countries should be put on operations research and the biomedical research effort of local medical schools should be limited to directed, collaborative research in regional or international programs.

From the development perspective, this is the desirable evolution of the experiment initiated by the U.S. National Institutes of Health ten years ago in supporting five International Centers for Medical Research and Training. These centers are primarily designed to enrich the teaching and research capabilities of U.S. medical and public health schools and thus serve the health needs of Americans. The program, basically financed by $500,000 per annum grants from the National Institute of Allergy and Infectious Diseases, currently supports centers at Kuala Lumpur, Malaysia, involving the University of California and University of Malaysia; at Calcutta, involving Johns Hopkins University and three Indian institutions; at Lahore, West Pakistan, involving the University of Maryland and the Lahore Institute of Hygiene; and at Cali, Colombia, involving Tulane University and the University of Valle. The program's greatest difficulty probably has been the recruitment of second and subsequent rounds of U.S. university staff members of the quality required. There also have been problems of local financial support and responsibility for direction of research programs. Nevertheless, the centers provide host countries a base for expanding and more integrated participation in national research programs or in international collaborative research concentrated on a common problem.

Some or all of the centers could, with additional financial support, become part of a network of research and training designed to serve the needs of the less developed countries. Their contribution to the training of Americans in health fields with the greatest shortages of skills and importance to development assistance programs could be substantially enlarged.

Conclusions for U.S. Technical Assistance

The U.S. medical and public health community has justly criticized the decline of health technical assistance in U.S. international programs over the past decade. AID did put its primary trust in the ultimate health-giving powers of general economic development. With the exception of war-related programs in Vietnam, AID tended to leave new health technical assistance activities to international agencies. Some critics suspected the agency of slighting health on the theory that to lower mortality rates would worsen the population crisis. There was no such official doctrine, nor would it have been rational in light of what is now known about the motivational and organizational keys to successful family planning programs. Nevertheless, the impression persisted.

General economic development, loosening the severe constraints in fiscal and human resources on health services, is fundamental to any long-term health strategy in low-income countries. However, at their projected economic growth rates most of these countries will continue to be desperately short of resources for complete health coverage for the rest of this century. Tools and techniques for stretching their resources must be found if poor or remote majorities are to have the health protection now regarded as a human right.

A renewed and modernized U.S. technical assistance program should express this country's interest in people, its egalitarian philosophy, and its humanitarian concern for the disadvantaged. This is not to suggest random, sentimental acts of charity. Technical assistance will make little impact on the enormous social deficits of poverty-stricken countries unless it concentrates on strategic multipliers of those countries' indigenous capabilities to cope with their problems.

The overriding health need of less developed countries is to raise continually the productivity of their publicly managed health delivery systems, both preventive and curative, so as to better serve the neglected majority. In broad, familiar terms, it is to economize on the scarcest resources so as to get the greatest health benefits. This common objective transcends the diversity of health problems and responses among countries. It suggests, therefore, a basic outlook for planning international health cooperation, whether in research or education or sectoral planning or operations.

This common diagnosis demands uncommon, imaginative prescriptions, new technology, a new breed of manager-consultants in health service, and a small army of middle-level technical manpower. It implies a national will, among both the political and medical leaders of a developing country, to put the interests of the many above those of the few in the allocation of health resources. And it requires consistent action within a broad national health strategy by public institutions that are outside the narrowly defined health field.

The problems and existing machinery for solving them point to the approaches for a new U.S. technical assistance program. The United States must first be sure that it has something of value to offer the developing countries, in which it has a comparative advantage internationally, and that these skills can be organized for sensitive collaboration with the health institutions of those countries. American medical schools, professional associations, specialized organizations in health-related fields, and public and private research agencies must work with the U.S. technical assistance agency in this task. It will take a broad, nationwide effort to rekindle the interest of the most qualified American experts and institutions and to organize pools of technical resources for cooperation with the developing countries. The initiative cannot be left entirely to the aid agencies.

The work need engage only a very small fraction of the total U.S. health manpower or facilities at any one time, but these must be the best. A few will have to be kept on a standby status for responding to requests, particularly for short-term professional consultants. Some can remain at their home bases, with only occasional travel, while participating in research projects, providing advanced training to specialists from abroad, or opening their laboratories to visiting researchers from developing countries.

The case for participation by U.S. health institutions rests partly on the proposition that the country will benefit from learning how to make health systems for lower income groups more efficient and by reducing tropical health threats to U.S. commerce, investment, and travel. On these grounds the Department of Health, Education, and Welfare (HEW) and its Public Health Service and National Institutes of Health should be enabled to use their resources to improve U.S. centers of training in international health and to apply more of their research capacity to tropical disease prevention and therapy.

The National Academy of Sciences should use its unique position to orient U.S. medical research toward filling critical knowledge gaps in the health programs of the tropical developing countries. Its Advisory Committee on Tropical Medicine recommended in 1962 that the academy organize and coordinate a "national program for research in tropical health" to focus the various U.S. public and private research efforts related to this field.[7] No great increase in overall funding of U.S. research would be required. The suggestion has lain dormant because of lack of administrative funds or enthusiasm on the part of some of those who would be coordinated. The U.S. technical assistance agency should consider reviving this scheme and financing the National Academy's administrative costs if necessary.

Program activities should largely be determined by requests

7. Ibid., p. 293.

of developing countries. The health and development authorities of a developing country will need to know, however,
which among the many assistance agencies can readily provide
what kinds of expert help in what way. An assistance agency
must have a conception of its own interests and fields of specialization in order to build a staff and mobilize a pool of external collaborators that will give it an identifiable niche and
reputation. In the United States, nongovernmental institutions usually cannot take initiatives to establish collaborative
arrangements with foreign institutions without knowing
whether the official technical assistance agency will support
some part of the effort.

The sensible way to establish the main program thrusts or
specialties of the new U.S. program is through consultation
with the developing countries, international agencies, and
principal U.S. health institutions. The program will evolve
through experience in meeting shifting requirements. Nevertheless, it is possible to identify several promising fields of U.S.
specialization.

The United States can provide individual experts or teams
to help in a health sector survey, preferably in concert with an
international lending agency interested in financing systematic
correction of the weaknesses identified by the survey. Ideally,
the survey should include nutrition and population program
services. It will be most productive if conducted under the
auspices of the national development planning authorities.
The product should not be just another report but should include at least the first stages of specific technical and capital
project designs. One of the great needs of the developing countries in health and other fields is the identification and design
of projects appropriate for international assistance. The host
country will ultimately decide whether to seek U.S. technical
assistance to carry out the recommended projects.

The United States can supply both advisers and interim staff members to help establish health sector planning units in governmental development policy and planning agencies and in health ministries. These units should have operational research and evaluation functions as well as programming capacity. In some countries they will be the best, if not only, means of bringing about a reorientation of local research toward the problems of health delivery services or sponsoring collaborative experimental work on service innovations.

The United States can support health research and dissemination of its results. Preference should be given to applied and operational research designed to improve public health services, health manpower training and utilization, and technological means of preventing major diseases of low-income tropical countries. Participating U.S. research institutions should make extraordinary efforts to collaborate with researchers of the developing countries—always in the case of operational research and wherever feasible in the case of laboratory work and field testing of biomedical tools.

The United States can assist in establishment of operational health research centers and programs in the developing countries, offering staff and budgetary support for an interim period if needed. The main U.S. contribution will be in teaching through example the methodology of applied social or operational research.

The United States may be able to strengthen the teaching of community health in medical schools of developing countries and the training of auxiliary personnel in special schools or adjuncts of medical schools. Perhaps the most important means of raising the productivity of health services are these training programs. Yet it is not at all clear that the United States has comparative advantage in work on such training programs. The developing countries need large cadres of subprofessional auxiliaries or assistant health officers to achieve "a much greater outreach of service at lower cost . . . a more effective utilization of scarce professional manpower, and the introduction of innovations and new programs that otherwise would not be possible."[8] Their medical education should produce a physician committed to public service and prepared to manage health services and professionally supervise auxiliaries and technicians. The U.S. competence in these fields lies in schools of public health and nonformal education systems, such as those of industrial companies and the armed forces, rather than conventional medical education.

General support of medical colleges does not merit priority in future U.S. programs. The United States can, however, help in special programs to expose health ministry and medical school staffs to the fundamentals of economic development and development agency administrators or economists to community medicine. This might be accomplished by arranging interdisciplinary programs for graduate students in health and economics at U.S. universities. The aim would be to remove parochial blinders, better equipping this professional elite for the comprehensive roles that many of them must play in developing countries. They must, for example, decide continually, in one way or another, whether to use intensive efforts to try to save one life while the same resources used in other ways might save one hundred.[9] Here, as in other fields, the guiding principle of technical assistance is to help establish the means for reasoned local judgment and more efficient use of scarce resources.

8. N. R. E. Fendall, "The Training of Auxiliary Personnel," in Willoughby Latham and Anne Newberry (eds.), *Community Medicine— Teaching, Research, and Health Care* (Appleton-Century-Crofts, Meredith Corp., 1970).

9. B. Abel-Smith, "What Priority Health? Tasks and Priorities in the Organization of Medical Services," in Moshe Prywes and A. Michael Davies (eds.), *Health Problems in Developing Countries*, Proceedings of the Fourth Rehovoth Conference (New York: Grune & Stratton, 1968).

CHAPTER FIVE

Research Keys to the Population Problem

POPULATION PROGRAMS, the newest field of development, demonstrate most clearly the case for a long-term, research-oriented, and collaborative system of technical assistance. Because it will take another decade or more of intense
effort to bring population growth within tolerable bounds in
most of the developing countries, the assistance must be long
term. It should be oriented toward research because the whole
movement to restrain human reproduction through community action is a series of social and biological experiments; success depends heavily on devising better and more diverse contraceptive technology, more efficient methods of program
operation and staffing, and more effective means of popular
education and motivation. Collaboration is important because
there are few models of successful programs to copy and no
assurance that their methods are widely applicable; the lessons
of trial and error must be promptly exchanged internationally
to save the critical element, time.

Family planning or population programs, it should be clear
from the outset, involve the whole complex of development.
Certainly technical assistance is not enough. Both general development assistance on a large scale and budgetary support
to population programs are likely to be required by countries
acutely afflicted by excessive population growth and attempting to bring it down to tolerable limits. To assume or wish

otherwise is to ignore the political reality that a government in office today is investing in the longer term future—usually of a successor regime—when it reallocates its very limited resources to a serious, intensive population program.

Population programs are still in their formative stages. No one can define with confidence today what mixture of public and private actions will prove most efficient and acceptable in regulating population growth in all societies or even in a single country. There will be wide variations among countries and within large ones, as well as changes over time, reflecting distinctive and sometimes rapidly changing political, religious, or other cultural factors and economic conditions. Some governments may confine their action indefinitely to gradual expansion of opportunities for parents to determine how many children they will have, without attempting to influence their decisions. Others may move promptly into a complex of social measures designed to achieve optimum population growth through regulation as soon as possible. Typically, the distinction between simple family planning and complex population programs is likely to be blurred or shifting.

The basic roles of foreign assistance in these great social experiments are twofold: to participate in and accelerate the process of finding out exactly what works with what costs and efficiency in controlling fertility in each environment; and to provide financial and technical means of continually improving both the initially and ultimately selected fertility-control measures. The functions overlap. The program administrator must get on with the job, using the limited knowledge and tools available, while improving the knowledge, administrative and technical means, and collateral support for a more effective job in the future. Helping him reach the next stage of greater effectiveness sooner is the challenge to international technical assistance.

The First Decade

The foundations for more systematic action were laid in the 1960s, when the world awoke to the population explosion and began trying to check it. At first only a few political leaders of the developing countries were willing to grapple with the reality that their populations—growing by 2.5 to over 3 percent annually—were multiplying at three or more times the rates that nations industrializing during the nineteenth century had had to cope with. By the end of the decade the problem was commonly recognized and resistance to action on it was collapsing.

Financial and development leaders were among the first to see the price of high population growth as it eroded hard-won gains in production and social services. In unbalanced populations, nearly half below productive ages, the average worker in developing countries was attempting to support almost twice as many dependents as his counterpart in the industrialized countries.

With the realization that quality of population is more important than quantity in achieving national greatness, nationalistic opposition to checking population growth began to crumble. Theological opposition weakened as evidence mounted that the alternative to contraception often was abortion—even less acceptable, often unsafe and illegal—and that denial of public birth-control services to the desperate poor discriminated in favor of the rich. Ideologues of varied hues were given pause on learning that when it came to birthrates, communist Eastern Europe and capitalist Western Europe were almost indistinguishable among the lowest in the world. Finally, political leaders discovered that many of their people were ahead of them in favoring government action to help relieve mothers and children of the health and nutrition handicaps of too-frequent childbirth.

Gradually, the warnings of demographers and economists began to be heard. The primary issue for developing countries was not "overpopulation" (although ecologists in the West were warning of this, too) but the speed of population growth in relation to the speed with which economic resources could be developed. Population and development were interdependent parts of the same equation. Empty lands and the natural potential for feeding a much larger population were of little help if consumption was outrunning the capital formation, investment, and current budgets needed to develop and use natural and human resources.

Some of the more development-minded governments began to respond to these lessons. India, which had taken a faltering lead in the early 1950s, revived and reorganized its family planning program in 1963–65. Pakistan, beginning in 1960 and reorganizing for a major effort in the mid-1960s, demonstrated the vital role of top-level political leadership in getting a program under way. South Korea, mainland China, Taiwan, Tunisia, Singapore, the United Arab Republic, Mauritius, Ceylon, Kenya, Malaysia, Nepal, and Jamaica followed. By the end of the decade, twenty-five nations containing 73 percent of the total population of less developed countries in Asia, Africa, and Latin America (or twenty-four with about 60 percent if mainland China is excluded) had official policies and programs in support of family planning.[1]

The shift in governmental attitudes was dramatic. For example, the government of Ghana, some of whose diplomatic representatives had been critical of the United States for pro-

1. *Population and Family Planning Programs: A Factbook*, Reports on Population/Family Planning, 2 (Population Council and International Institute for the Study of Human Reproduction, Columbia University, July 1970), Tables 3, 6.

moting birth control in aid programs, adopted a model population policy in 1969. Its opening paragraphs declared:

The population of Ghana is the nation's most valuable resource.
It is both the instrument and the objective of national development. The protection and enhancement of its welfare is the Government's first responsibility. When that welfare is threatened, the
Government must act.

The welfare of the nation is now endangered by a subtle, almost
imperceptible demographic change. During the past three or four
decades the death rate has been slowly falling, permitting more
children to survive into adulthood and adding years to the life ex-
pectancy of our people. But while the death rate has been falling,
there has been no noticeable change in the birth rate. Patterns of
high fertility that were appropriate, perhaps even necessary, in an
era of high mortality are continuing in a time when they have become inappropriate and unnecessary. Unless birth rates can be
brought down to parallel falling death rates, Ghana's population
will climb at a rate dangerous to continuing prosperity, and the
children of the next few generations will be born into a world
where their very numbers may condemn them to life-long poverty.

. . . The basis of concern about Ghana's population is not that
the country is presently over-populated but that the growth rate is
so high that it is already retarding economic progress thus frustrat-
ing national development aspirations and producing a demographic situation that could have serious social, economic, and perhaps political consequences.[2]

The government of the staunchly Catholic Philippines
adopted early in 1970 a population policy and program that
encompassed not only provision of information, services, and
persuasion but also "specific and quantitative population
goals."[3] In Central and South America, the twin deterrents of
church opposition and the "empty lands" delusion had limited
the family planning movement to either private and initially

2. "Population Planning for National Progress and Prosperity," Government of Ghana Population Policy, issued March 1969.
3. "Statement on Population Policy and Program," Commission on
Population, Republic of the Philippines, 1969.

surreptitious efforts or extremely cautious governmental support. However, the climate began to change before the end of the decade. A Latin American political leader lectured his hemispheric neighbors—albeit privately—in the fall of 1970 on the theme that development and population programs must be pursued simultaneously in countries confronting both high chronic unemployment and high birthrates. Development doctrine in Latin America increasingly recognized population growth as the source of the region's enormous demands for new jobs. Latin America's predominantly Catholic women told political leaders something in their rising private purchase of contraceptives.

Almost as important as political change in triggering the initiation of official family planning programs was the emergence of a new contraceptive technology. The inexpensive plastic intrauterine device (IUD), particularly, offered the means of long-term but reversible contraception on which a mass program could be built. Two of the more successful programs, in Taiwan and South Korea, were largely built on the IUD. "Indirectly, by giving national programs some hope of success, the IUD stimulated a wholly new level of effort, improved the morale of family planning workers from the top down, and, most importantly, brought about the development of family planning organizations in a form and magnitude not previously known. Whatever new contraceptive method emerges over the next years will benefit from the network of doctors, administrators, and field workers now in existence thanks largely to this device."[4]

When the IUD's limitations—expulsions and therapeutic terminations and low appeal to younger mothers of fewer chil-

4. Bernard Berelson, "National Family Planning Programs: Where We Stand," in S. J. Behrman, L. Corsa, and R. Freedman (eds.), *Sesquicentennial Proceedings, Fertility and Family Planning: A World View* (University of Michigan Press, 1969).

dren—began to dampen enthusiasm for it as the technological panacea, the availability of steroid hormone pills at greatly reduced prices reinvigorated lagging programs in some countries.[5] (Concern over the pill's side effects, however minor in relation to the high risks of childbirth in most parts of most developing countries, has limited the use of oral contraceptives.) In India, sterilization has maintained some momentum in the program while the enormous job of building its administrative structure proceeded. In Japan and Eastern Europe, simpler and safer methods of abortion have reinforced changes in laws and social attitudes and opened new avenues to fertility control.

Lessons of Early Experience

One of the key lessons of the first decade is the critical role of technology in energizing and popularizing birth-control programs. The introduction of new birth-control methods creates increased interest in all means of regulating fertility. As new methods of spacing and limiting births become commonly known and endorsed by medical, religious, and political authorities they appear to increase use of the whole range of fertility-control methods.

A less encouraging lesson is the significant part that personal motivation and program administration must play in programs using today's technology. These are major limitations to achievement of the goals of full coverage of the programs or sustained reduction in the birthrate.

Demand for reliable, convenient, and cheap means of birth control proved to be far greater than the 10 or 15 percent of married women in the reproductive ages who were thought to

5. Taiwan and Korea were more effective in dealing with the problem of IUD terminations than countries with less well-trained field staffs.

be practicing primitive, ineffective, or costly methods when
the programs began. Early surveys taken in the pioneer countries, before their family planning promotional campaigns
could have had much impact, indicated that 40–60 percent of
the married women or couples who had three children wanted
to stop there, and the desire for birth control rose as the number of children rose. In India, after wide promotional efforts
but limited rural delivery of family planning services, 90 percent of the rural couples surveyed who had four or more children said they did not wish to have additional children. (How
strongly they felt this may be another question.) One-third of
India's reproductive-age couples fall in this group. Urban couples said they wanted to limit their families, on the average, to
three children.[6]

The most important lesson of the first decade of family
planning programs is that they do speed the decline in birthrates—especially among older couples with larger numbers of
children. Success has been in rough relationship with the scale
of coverage and duration of service efforts. Measurement of
program effectiveness is very difficult, however, because of poor
demographic data, the unknown contribution of other influences, and uncertainty about the extent to which the program
merely substitutes more modern for traditional methods of
regulating fertility.

Korean government studies corroborated by some American
research sampling attribute about half of the 10-point decline
(from 42 to 32 per 1,000) in South Korea's crude birthrate
between 1961 and 1969 to the official IUD program. That program had reached about 50 percent of the married women of
reproductive ages by 1969 and about 22 percent of them had
participated, for the world's best record of IUD usage. The annual budget for the program, including foreign assistance, had

6. Statement by the representative of the Government of India at the
India Consortium Meeting, at Stockholm, November 1969.

been relatively high in relation to per capita income for the last half of the decade.

Hong Kong recorded a decline in its crude birthrate from over 35 per 1,000 to about 20 per 1,000 and Taiwan from over 37 to about 28 per 1,000 during the 1960s. Studies attempting to isolate the role of Hong Kong's Family Planning Association program credit it with a "signficant" share of this remarkable decline.[7] In Taiwan, fertility was found to have declined 30 percentage points more among IUD acceptors than among comparable nonacceptors.[8] Taiwan and Hong Kong during the late 1960s made a particularly encouraging advance—not matched in the less advantaged countries of southern Asia—in the proportions of younger women with fewer children included among IUD acceptors, indicating that "the influence spreads from older women with the immediate problem to those who must anticipate the problem."[9]

The role of technology may be seen in the fact that during the 1960s, the accelerated decline in overall birthrate in Taiwan, which did not add oral contraceptives to its program until 1969, was among women over 30; they account for only one-fourth of the country's births.[10] The decline in fertility in Central America, where orals are the main method, does not omit the younger women. Whether this comparison suggests that the pill is a ready answer to the problem of motivating younger parents with few children to practice birth control in less lit-

7. Ronald Freedman and others, *Hong Kong: The Continuing Fertility Decline*, 1967, Studies in Family Planning (New York: Population Council, August 1969).

8. L. P. Chow and others, *Demographic Impact of an IUD Program*, Studies in Family Planning (Population Council, September 1969).

9. Ronald Freedman, "Social Research and Programs for Reducing Birth Rates" (paper prepared for conference on population at Villa Serbelloni, Italy, April 1970).

10. Thomas Merrick, "Future Expansion of Population Programs" (resource paper for AID Spring Review of Population Programs, May 1970; processed).

erate countries with weaker health services is yet to be determined.

In India the proportions of married couples reached by the program and using contraceptives vary among the states and are generally highest in those with the most extensive geographic coverage and vigorous family planning staffs. In Punjab, Kerala, and Maharashtra, with the more complete area coverage and 48, 35, and 33 percent, respectively, of all couples reached, the achievements were close to those of Korea and Taiwan in the same year (1969). About 11 million Indian couples (out of 97 million) were recorded in 1969 as acceptors of program services, of which about 6.5 million were sterilized and 3 million protected at one time by the IUD. The total acceptors were reported by the Indian government to be rising in 1969 at a rate of nearly 3 million a year. The net increase in effective birth-control practice is smaller than that, however, because of a substantial but not fully known number of dropouts from the IUD and irregular users of conventional contraceptives. There was evidence that the Indian program was not gaining new users as rapidly as the program budget was increasing.

In fact, the cost of each birth averted appears to rise as older programs reach out to more remote areas and less highly motivated couples (see Table 5-1). Improvements in the quality of services, including a broader range of contraceptive methods and more intensive motivational efforts, should check the decline in cost-effectiveness.

India's experience, though not fully measured, offers some useful lessons on administrative and motivational problems and some clues to the ultimate cost of achieving fertility reductions in the more populous and predominantly rural nations. India's task is enormous: to establish a network of nearly 50,000 service centers effectively reaching reproductive-age couples in 3,000 cities and towns and over 550,000 villages; to train, assign, and support more than 150,000 professional, technical, and administrative persons to staff these stations; to engage private groups, volunteer agents, commercial enterprises, communications media, and other molders of opinion in a multitude of supporting efforts; and to increase financial allocations to the effort rapidly, at the expense of other urgently needed social services or more visible and immediate popular benefits.

The Indian program to reduce birthrates has fallen behind its original optimistic targets. The government expects to reach the initial goal of 25 births per 1,000 by about the end of the 1970s instead of 1976. At the end of the current five-year plan in 1974, it hopes that more complete (but still not intensive) nationwide coverage will have reduced the birthrate from the mid-1960s estimate of over 40 per 1,000 to about 32. This would yield a population growth rate of about 2 percent in the mid-1970s, assuming a further decline in the death rate from the late 1960s level of 14 to around 12 per 1,000. By the end of the 1970s, the population growth rate would be down to about 1.5 percent.[11]

The more extensive demographic studies now under way should reveal more accurately how well the program is meeting these demographic objectives. Enough information has been obtained, however, to persuade Indian government and foreign assistance agencies to increase spending on the program and press for more rapid completion of program coverage and qualitative improvements.

India's annual program budget is scheduled to rise from about $56 million (exclusive of direct foreign aid) in 1969–70 to about $100 million by 1974, when service will have been established in about 75 percent of the projected rural centers and virtually all cities and towns. Gross annual expenditures

11. Statement of Indian government representative at Stockholm.

TABLE 5-1. *Family Planning Program Performance, Selected Countries, 1961–70*

Program characteristic and country	1961	1962	1963	1964	1965	1966	1967	1968	1969	1970
Program expenditure per eligible couple (dollars)										
Chile	..	..	..	0.17	0.31	0.79	0.75	1.22	n.a.	n.a.
India	0.04	0.07	0.07	0.12	0.22	0.24	0.44	0.48	0.60	n.a.
Korea	..	0.10	0.17	0.32	0.39	0.70	0.73	1.00	0.81	n.a.
Malaysia	..	..	..	..	..	..	0.41	0.72	0.90	1.02
Pakistan	..	..	..	..	..	0.35	0.56	0.76	n.a.	n.a.
Taiwan	..	..	..	0.09	0.33	0.29	0.33	0.42	0.45	0.54
Tunisia	..	..	..	..	..	..	..	1.22	1.16	n.a.
Percent of eligible couples in program										
Chile	..	..	..	1.2	3.9	7.1	12.0	14.8	n.a.	n.a.
India	0.4	0.5	1.1	1.6	3.0	4.5	6.4	8.4	9.9	n.a.
Korea	..	0.1	0.7	8.1	13.2	18.8	20.4	21.2	25.8	27.1
Malaysia	..	..	..	..	..	..	0.9	5.4	7.2	7.1
Pakistan	..	..	..	..	..	2.8	7.9	14.0	17.8	n.a.
Taiwan	..	..	..	2.3	6.2	8.9	12.0	14.0	14.9	16.3
Tunisia	..	..	..	0.3	1.8	3.2	3.7	4.6	5.7	6.8

Percent of expected births averted by program

Chile	…	…	…	…	1.2	4.4	8.0	13.5	16.4	n.a.
India	0.2	0.4	0.5	1.0	1.5	2.9	4.2	6.1	7.9	9.2
Korea	…	…	0.1	0.6	6.2	10.5	15.2	16.2	16.7	20.7
Malaysia	…	…	…	…	…	…	…	0.9	5.6	7.4
Pakistan	…	…	…	…	…	…	2.3	6.5	11.6	14.9
Taiwan	…	…	…	…	1.9	5.0	6.9	9.2	10.3	10.5
Tunisia	…	…	…	…	0.3	2.0	3.5	3.9	5.0	6.1

Expenditure per birth averted (dollars)

Chile	11.54	…	13.99	11.03	17.71	10.67	16.23	n.a.	n.a.
India	…	16.35	12.26	10.88	8.01	8.67	10.60	15.60	n.a.
Korea	…	47.43	7.79	7.66	9.36	11.70	17.25	10.26	n.a.
Malaysia	…	…	…	…	…	71.48	24.07	32.46	45.83
Pakistan	…	…	…	…	28.67	16.62	10.68	n.a.	n.a.
Taiwan	…	…	10.04	17.30	13.76	12.73	15.66	16.67	17.88
Tunisia	…	…	…	…	…	…	51.91	38.68	n.a.

Source: U.S. Agency for International Development (AID), unpublished tabulations, 1972.
n.a.: Not available.

per couple will rise from 50 cents to about $1 (or less than 20 cents per capita) over this period.

A series of cost-effectiveness studies by Pennsylvania State University found that India was getting some 14 million "couple years of protection" in 1968–69 at a cost of $3.10 per couple in total program expenditures.[12] Assuming that one birth is averted annually by every three or four "couple years of protection,"[13] the Indian program averted about 3.5 million births in 1968–69 at a cost of about $12 each.

India's costs of averting births (using its present limited range of methods) seem likely to rise as the program attempts to reach more remote, younger, and otherwise less motivated couples. This prospect is implied in its current five-year plan. If the crude birthrate declines as projected, India will have about 25 million fewer births than would have occurred at the 1968–69 birthrate. By 1974 the annual decline would be only about 3.5 million births at the 1969 rate of reduction. The cost of each birth averted under these projections ranges from $17 (if all credit for sustaining and increasing the decline in crude birthrate is claimed for the program) to about $40 (if credit is claimed only for the additional decline in birthrate after 1969). While not properly comparable with the $12 estimate for 1968–69, calculated retrospectively, these figures suggest a trend.

Is this too high a price to pay in developing countries struggling with high fertility, capital shortages, labor surpluses, and a huge backlog of unmet social and economic investment de-

12. Warren Robinson and others, "A Cost-Effectiveness Analysis of Selected National Family Planning Programs," a Report of Phase 2 of the Penn State–USAID Population Project (Pennsylvania State University, December 1969; processed). Costs of a couple year of protection in Chile were $6.95; in Tunisia, $20.00; Pakistan, $2.79; Korea, $2.48; and Taiwan, $2.21 (all based on 1968 reports except Korea where 1967 was used).

13. Berelson, "National Family Planning Programs."

mands? It is reasonable to assume that in such countries a birth averted ultimately saves at least twice a country's per capita income. With the expenditure of about $100 million in 1974, if India averted a conservatively calculated 3 million births that year by means of its family planning program, it would ultimately save about $600 million—an undiscounted 6:1 yield. This, of course, does not take into account many intangible benefits to the families concerned. Few alternative investments offering high social returns promise such a favorable cost–benefit ratio. But many alternatives offer greater certainty of achieving less spectacular returns, and sooner.

The Next Phase

The example set by the pioneer countries will have an important bearing on how far and fast the movement to control population growth spreads in the 1970s. If they succeed in sustaining crude birthrate declines of a point or more annually at costs as low as 20 to 25 cents per capita, without coercion, serious population programs are likely to win a firm place in national development plans of many more countries. If they falter or their cost-effectiveness declines steeply, the late starters in this field are more likely to settle for token or passive programs, forfeiting time and compounding their future problems. In this sense, particularly, the success of the pacesetters is a matter of global concern.

Early identification and correction of shortcomings in the more advanced programs thus becomes doubly important. The decennial census and the current or planned evaluative studies should provide a firmer basis for measuring progress, spotting weaknesses, and prescribing improvements in the established programs. However, some problems that already are plainly visible raise serious doubts that a point-a-year pace in birthrate reductions can be sustained through the decade by simple expansion of presently constituted programs.

The main problems are in program staffing and administration, weighting the multitude of social factors that affect or might be brought to bear on fertility trends, and working with the limited contraceptive means available. All these problems intertwine. They compound weaknesses in political will and complicate efforts to fix a reasonable allocation of resources to population programs within a national development strategy. They will become more apparent as programs attempt to move past the relatively easy first stages where they respond to the active demands of over-thirty parents of four or more children. This is a big market, far from satisfied in India and Pakistan and only beginning to be reached in the newer programs, but its satisfaction takes a country only part way down the road toward reducing population growth to tolerable limits. The essential breakthrough—in shifting the motivations of younger couples with fewer children to delay and space childbearing and reduce their concepts of a desirable family size—has not yet been made. (Urbanized, progressive Hong Kong, Singapore, and parts of Malaysia seem to be exceptions, but their advantages are not readily applicable to large or lesser developed countries.) Introduction of oral contraceptives seems to help narrow the motivational gap, but at the beginning of the 1970s it still had not been tried on a mass scale in the more traditional societies.

Only plausible assumptions can be made about what it takes to shift motivations toward lower fertility in the great variety of circumstances existing in "traditional" or "transitional" societies. Economic and social modernization historically has paralleled reductions in birthrates, but in the shorter run rising family incomes and better health may increase net population growth rates. It is the function of population programs to accelerate reductions in birthrates and thus make a positive contribution to economic and social progress, rather than wait for the overburdened processes of modernization to overcome the population problems. Improvement of population programs depends heavily on systematic research and experimental projects to acquire practical knowledge of the complex of social factors at work on fertility trends and of ways to influence them effectively.

Common sense and some empirical evidence suggest that convenient and timely access to trustworthy birth control information and services can activate latent motivations. A massive and intensive network of neighborhood public and private family planning centers, or more comprehensive fertility-control centers and private distribution outlets may be what is needed. But common sense and official caution suggest that the service must be professionally competent if the clientele is to be held and enlarged through times when new contraceptive practices prove unpopular or motivations are lower. (Side effects of new contraceptives could undermine public and political support for population programs, especially if the health professions were alienated in the process of introducing a new contraceptive rather than being a party to the decision and program.) Concern about proper medical supervision has slowed the pace of establishing family planning networks and in some countries has restricted the variety of fertility controls offered. Most of the developing countries are years to decades away from extending professional health services to the bulk of their people.

One theoretical solution is to sweep away the organizational, manpower, and budgetary obstacles and create a universal health and population service, coupled with subsidized private sale of contraceptives, that continues the intensity of efforts specifically directed at birth control. Several countries are attempting to move in this direction through greater use of subprofessional manpower, and more research on this approach is urgently needed. If and where it proves feasible, it will require substantial increases in foreign technical and financial assistance.

In the meantime, momentum may be maintained by additional family planning services that are independent of the rural health clinic system. Existing hospitals, traditional midwifery services, and maternity clinics can be used to provide family planning advice and services immediately after childbirth. Such a "postpartum" approach exploits momentarily high interest in limiting or delaying further pregnancies and should be relatively efficient in converting fertile mothers to reliable contraception. More knowledge about continuation rates among postpartum contraceptive acceptors is essential to testing the cost-effectiveness of such a program. The Population Council is leading an experimental study of this question in fourteen countries.

With improved delivery systems and motivational efforts, population programs will still fall short of their goals until a much broader technology, less dependent on doctors, is produced. A greater variety of more easily and safely used contraceptives would relieve many of the motivational as well as administrative constraints on the programs. Satisfied users are the best promoters of the program, and the reverse is at least equally true. A wide variety of contraceptive means is required to satisfy the many age groups, diverse living conditions, cultural taboos, and medical or pharmaceutical standards in the developing countries. The prospect of continuing scarcity or inconvenience of medical service heightens the need for a diversity of safe, self-administered means of birth control that do not require medical supervision. A complete technology would include a more reliable rhythm method (although this method would continue to depend on self-discipline), better means of reversible sterilization, and clinical abortion facilities.[14] In the meantime, some of the coverage gaps could be closed by the addition of oral contraceptives, under reasonable and workable controls, in programs that thus far have shunned them.

Given the difficulties and limitations of today's family planning programs, what can be done outside these programs to accelerate declines in fertility? Some governments are trying to ease the motivational constraints through their educational systems and communications media. Several countries are beginning to modify pronatalist policies expressed in their tax exemptions for dependents, family allowances, and welfare programs. A great many other schemes have been advanced. Some would impose penalties for exceeding certain family sizes or offer financial inducements to encourage contraception; others would raise the minimum age of marriage, substitute pension systems for the traditional "social security" of male children, promote education of women and their employment outside the home, or tinker with the nature of marriage and the family itself.

In cataloging and evaluating these schemes "beyond family planning," Berelson notes the infeasibility of many, the uncertain cost-effectiveness of all, and the serious ethical issues raised by those that contain elements of compulsion or penalize the innocent and the poor.[15] Nevertheless, some measures to heighten motivations in support of population programs probably will be required, including more intensive public education, financial inducements, and—for symbolic more than

14. India adopted a policy of clinical abortion-on-demand in early 1972. Its advocates hoped that fee-paying demand would be strong enough to encourage thousands of doctors to establish abortion and follow-up contraceptive clinics throughout the country.

15. Bernard Berelson, *Beyond Family Planning*, Studies in Family Planning (Population Council, February 1969).

practical reasons—the elimination of the more blatant pronatalist laws and policies. Very discriminating research and
evaluation will be required to offer useful guidance on whether
any of the more attractive suggestions are worth the financial,
social, or political cost.

The "necessary" combination of measures for the next phase
of population programs obviously depends on the goals of individual nations. Originally, family planning programs were
designed simply to get started in the easiest, least contentious
ways. The evolution to complex objectives, including health,
demographic, and broader development targets, has been faster
than most observers believed possible five years ago, and there
have been virtually no political reversals. The guiding concept
of individual freedom of choice has been preserved; compulsion has been rejected as wrong, unworkable, or both. For the
foreseeable future, this doctrine will remain a crucial condition of international assistance to population programs. Fortunately, it does not impose any strong constraint on the adoption and achievement of ambitious demographic goals in the
1970s.

Neither the population a nation will ultimately consider its
tolerable limit nor the fertility-control measures required to
meet that limit can be predicted. The longer action to reduce
growth rates is delayed, however, the bigger will be the final
population. For some nations, it already is too late to decide to
stablize their populations eventually at twice their present
numbers. The momentum of the demographic avalanche
makes it later than most people think. It takes about three
generations to shift from a severely unbalanced population
with high proportions of young people, as in most low-income
countries, to a balanced one. In the meantime, there will be
more births than deaths. The lag between the time a country
cuts its fertility to a simple replacement level (about two chil-

dren per couple or close to a net reproduction rate of 1.00) and the time its population ceases to grow will be fifty to sixty years. In the interim, its population will at least double the starting size, as is illustrated in Table 5-2.

The Research Agenda

The United States' greatest contribution to national population programs has been in creating and providing new contraceptive technology. The pivotal importance of further technological advances indicates that this is the area in which the United States and other technically advanced nations can most usefully invest in development assistance.

Embodied technology is one of three essential components of a population program. Strengthening the other two—service delivery systems and motivation to use the service—also depends on technological and social knowledge that can best be acquired from research or operational experiments. As programs advance to more complex goals and costs rise, the need grows for demographic facts, measurement of results, isolation of social and psychological causes and effects, and certain knowledge of the efficiency of alternative program compositions and delivery systems. Assistance in establishing and buttressing social science research in countries undertaking population programs can yield high returns where it is both welcome and sharply problem-oriented.

In both these fields of population research, technological and social, the range of potentially useful study and experimentation is vastly greater than available combinations of funds, talent, and management capacity. Specialists and their special theories clamor for support. Immediate operational questions compete with longer term needs for basic knowl-

TABLE 5-2. *Projected Population Growth in Selected Countries during Efforts to Reach Stationary Population Levels*

Item	Chile	Mexico	Ghana	Tunisia	Indonesia	Thailand
Estimated population, 1970 (millions)	10	50	9	5	120	37
Year during which population becomes stationary if it is assumed that net reproduction rate becomes 1.00[a] in the five-year period						
1980–85	2045	2040	2045	2040	2045	2045
1990–95	2050	2050	2050	2055	2050	2050
2000–2005	2060	2060	2060	2060	2060	2060
Estimated stationary population (millions) if it is assumed that net reproduction rate becomes 1.00[a] in the five-year period						
1980–85	19	110	18	11	238	77
1990–95	22	134	22	13	280	94
2000–2005	25	165	27	16	336	116

Source: AID; based on projections of the International Demographic Statistics Center, Population Division, U.S. Bureau of the Census.

a. A net reproduction rate of 1.00—and hence, eventually, a stationary population—implies that each woman in the population, on the average, bears one surviving daughter.

edge or ultimate solutions. Personnel and institutional limitations in the developing countries restrict social or behavorial research and operational experiments, which must be done locally in close conjunction with a national program. Contraceptive research, on the other hand, can much more easily be undertaken in the industrialized countries. It is potentially more useful to these countries, which are called upon to provide most of the funds and talent, than the related social science research. While special conditions in less developed countries dictate some of the criteria for improved contraceptives, these conditions obtain in clusters of countries. Consequently, research priorities can be globally determined, research capacity mobilized, and international collaboration arranged much more easily in the technological than in the social and operational fields.

Early leadership in identifying the main targets for population program research came primarily from a few American and Swedish workers in this new field, drawing largely on experience in eastern and southern Asia. The American group included specialists in the Population Council, the Ford, Rockefeller, and Worcester Foundations, population study centers at the Universities of Michigan and North Carolina and Johns Hopkins University, and individual demographers at several other universities. Subsequently, the U.S. Department of Health, Education, and Welfare and its National Institute of Child Health and Development, the Agency for International Development, the Salk Institute, and elements of the pharmaceutical industry assumed prominent roles, as well. Swedish contributions have stemmed from a group at the Karolinska Institute and Hospital and the Swedish International Development Agency. The United Nations Development Program, the World Health Organization, and the Organization for Economic Cooperation and Development (OECD) are beginning to acquire competence in this field.

Biomedical and Technological Research

Discussion and exchange of publications among this group of specialists have produced substantial agreement on the main requirements for research in reproductive biology and fertility-control technology. The broad purpose is clear, but by no means simple. It is the continuing development of an ever more complete array of contraceptives meeting the needs, preferences, or restrictions of various population groups; each type must be designed to rate high on most of these criteria: reliable, safe when self-administered, reversible, not dependent on frequent forethought, inexpensive. Obviously no single method is likely to be ideal on all counts for all users. However, one or more methods should at once be less frequently administered than the present generation of steroid hormone pills, more reliable than conventional contraceptives and rhythm, more attractive than IUDs to mothers just beginning their child-bearing and to those with physiological retention problems, and freer of side effects and less dependent on professional assistance than either the IUD or the present pill.

An HEW advisory panel convened in late 1969 grouped priority targets for contraceptive research under short-term and long-term approaches and the medical effects of contraceptives in use. For the short term, it saw a need for improved hormone methods of contraception, such as small doses of progestogen administered orally or through injection, implantation, or the like; low-dosage steroids, capable of inhibiting sperm function; improved IUDs, based on new bioengineering approaches and better understanding of the contraceptive function of such devices; simplified and reversible sterilization for men and women; and a more reliable rhythm method of birth control, possibly based on simple means of detecting hormone changes controlling ovulation. It recommended for long-term development a once-a-month menses-inducing or -regulating agent; a post-intercourse drug to prevent fertilization or implantation; and a modern male method of contraception. The study of medical effects of contraceptives in use should consider means of predicting the risk of thromboembolism in women using the estrogen-progestin pill; the possibility of a causal relationship between use of contraceptives and development of cancer; the significance of reported metabolic changes associated with use of the pill; the side effects of low-dose progestin medication; and the possibility of latent effects in children born after a mother suspends use of oral contraceptives.

Similar research priorities are suggested by other experts. The National Institutes of Health Center for Population Research, in its initial call for proposals in reproductive biology research, focused attention on four priority areas: "maturation and fertilizing capacity of spermatozoa; oviduct function and gamete transport; corpus luteum function and implantation; and biology of the pre-implantation ovum."

Professor Egon Diczfalusy of Karolinska Institute suggested that the most promising opportunities for new contraceptive research are in "interference with sperm motility; chemical sterilization of women; methods to induce endocervical hostility; agents interfering with corpus luteum function; and agent interfering with implantation and early embryonic development."[16]

The Agency for International Development, in its major allocations for contraceptive research, has supported improved design and testing of IUDs (principally by the Pathfinder Fund and collaborators, and beginning in 1970 by Battelle Memorial Institute); research on a once-a-month pill or other

16. Quoted by Oscar Harkavy and John Maier, "Research in Reproductive Biology and Contraceptive Technology: Present Status and Needs for the Future," in *Family Planning Perspectives*, Vol. 2, No. 3 (New York: Population Council, June 1970).

chemical application to assure maintenance of regular menses through interference with the corpus luteum (by the Population Council and associated researchers, by the Worcester Foundation, and by individual scientists); further focusing of the search for an ideal menses-inducing agent on a series of long-known fatty acids misnamed "prostaglandins" (by the Worcester Foundation and associated scientists, and by the Upjohn Company and the University of West Virginia); and analysis and synthesis of naturally occurring chemical agents called "gonadotropin releasing factors," that may be capable of inhibiting a single function in the chain of hormone-triggered events that make pregnancy possible (by Roger Guillemin, of the Salk Institute).

As many as thirty promising areas of research that might yield new contraceptive methods have been identified by the Population Council's Biomedical Division. The Carolina Population Center, in a review of knowledge gaps in reproductive biology, cited more than a score of poorly understood functions that may conceal effective approaches to fertility regulation.[17] One suggestion of areas not currently receiving much attention is the possibility of immunizing females against pregnancy by inducing the secretion of protective antibodies in the cervix. Others include temporary male sterilization through immunologic approaches and periodic chemical regulation.

Any new chemical contraceptives developed in programs just getting under way face years of testing in laboratory animals and in human clinical volunteers before their general release. Approval by the U.S. Food and Drug Administration may require that preparations using active ingredients that have not undergone thorough toxicity tests in animals be

17. Carolina Population Center, "Approaches to the Human Fertility Problem" (study prepared for the UN Advisory Committee on the Application of Science and Technology to Development, University of North Carolina at Chapel Hill, October 1968).

tested as long as ten years, perhaps five years for those that have substantial toxicity records. Promising new preparations sometimes pass many of their tests only to fail when side effects belatedly appear in test animals. This seems to be the fate of at least one low-dose progestin on which some hopes had been placed. If a new drug is released, the conditions attached by governmental health or drug-control authorities may be so restrictive as to frustrate plans for mass self-administration.

These notes of caution must temper the excitement aroused by reports of the prostaglandins' potential as the "ideal" fertility-control agent. Their potential has been demonstrated in clinical experiments conducted in Uganda, London, Stockholm, and elsewhere.[18] Initially, work focused on infusions to induce abortion without surgery and later on suppositories to restore menstruation in the early stages of a presumed pregnancy. In those societies where early-stage abortion is morally or legally acceptable, the availability of a self-administered means of either correcting occasional failures or replacing other methods of birth control with no more than monthly use comes close to the ideal technology. However, until much more is known about the safety of prostaglandins it is too early to celebrate.

Social and Operational Research

Program administrators have only gradually recognized their need for social science and operational research. In the beginning, programs could be based on crude estimates of population growth rates and some indications of popular demand for relief from unwanted pregnancies. As they grew on this unmet demand, progress could be measured by the numbers of acceptors and sample evidence of birthrate declines. Those who

18. *Annals of the New York Academy of Sciences*, Vol. 180 (April 1971).

insisted on the need for detailed information about what a program was doing and not doing, where it should concentrate for greatest effectiveness, or where and why it was least effective were sometimes regarded as self-serving academics, time-wasting kibitzers, or threateners of political embarrassment. Those who did recognize this need found that existing social and health research capacity was of little use in assessing operational requirements of population programs. As programs ran into problems or unexpected achievements, and as financial, training, or other administrative demands mounted, the need for more facts on which to measure results and chart the next course became apparent to all.

Most of the countries attempting or likely to attempt population programs start with very inadequate machinery for recording vital statistics, for collecting, collating, and analyzing census data, or for designing and carrying out surveys free of misleading errors. Some are handicapped by cultural inhibitions against prying into intimate sexual and psychological behavior. Training and research in demography or population dynamics is a new and poorly supported field in most universities. Those now able to organize social research have no baseline data to use for comparative purposes. The years of large-scale experimentation required to test some operational alternatives introduce delay and increase short-run costs.

By the end of the decade, serious efforts were being made by governments of the pioneer countries and some of the new starters to close the most serious knowledge gaps. Experts of several U.S. university population research centers were helping them, with support from foundations, AID, the World Health Organization, the U.S. Bureau of the Census, the Population Council, and other professional organizations. Expansion of local university research in demographic and behavorial aspects of population growth was financed by AID.

Nonetheless, it remained the judgment of Ronald Freedman, director of the University of Michigan Population Studies Center, that social research and evaluation efforts of most population programs were "grossly deficient" in "regular measurement of either fertility or birth control practice to indicate broad trends"; in determining what "social and economic factors affect actual fertility, norms about family size, and the practice of birth control"; and in knowledge of "important characteristics of the program clients" or "what happens to their birth control practice, fertility and well-being, especially after they leave the program"—knowledge obtained by comparison of "adequate samples of acceptors and comparable non-acceptors through the crucial stages of family life."[19]

The main categories of social information required by population programs include demographic facts and trends among discrete population groups, contraceptive practices within groups, and social, economic, and psychological factors affecting family size. Age of marriage, attitudes toward childbearing, and female employment outside the family are significant factors. If the key advantages of smaller families (education of children, health of children or mother, housing, psychological welfare) are to be stressed in motivational campaigns, social research must suggest what ought to be emphasized. Effects of government policies—whether or not they are intended to influence birthrates—must be known; welfare payments, housing and educational subsidies, family life or sex education, and equal employment rights for women are typical of policies that might alter family planning. Population growth and economic change affect each other; economic modernization, education, and other social changes may be reflected in fertility rates. Internal migrations and environmental response are aspects of population growth that ought to be

19. Freedman, "Social Research and Programs for Reducing Birth Rates."

measured. And effects of changes in child-spacing on family health and social progress should be calculated.

Operations research and evaluation encompass most of these searches and aim as well at providing answers to particular program problems. Among the common issues for operational research are how to determine achievable goals and relate program investments to them; the relative efficiency, costs, and requirements of alternative approaches to a program's goals; and how to reach new clients or keep older ones. Operational research also can test the effectiveness of different methods of recruiting, training, and compensating program staffs.

Cost-effectiveness studies can compare the benefits of a separate family planning delivery system versus a system integrated in the national health service. They can also contrast the costs and benefits of a narrowly targeted program, such as postpartum counseling and service or mobile clinics operating from district clinics and hospitals, and a more gradual expansion of village-level health/family planning services. Attitude-targets, listener-responses, and other factors determining the content and presentational methods of public education in support of family planning can be calculated, as can the costs and benefits of special approaches such as community television and radio, tie-ins with adult education programs, billboard advertising, and subsidized promotion of private contraceptive sales.

The duties and performance of program staff can be analyzed to find the best combination of economies in the use of scarce skills and the quantity, quality, and safety of the service provided. The correlation of different indexes of program progress can be tested. And responses can be evaluated to experiments such as incentive payments to program acceptors by government or private employers, payments to volunteer program promoters and client-finders, and free transportation for patients versus mobile clinics.

Research Management

In countries committed to serious population programs, knowledge gaps are being reduced and program possibilities are being examined. With action comes a problem familiar to development administration: how to mobilize and enhance existing capacities—typically little used and poorly managed—to do the research in close support of national programs.

The social and operational research agenda in any country will be awesome, and especially in countries with a frail data base or diverse cultural conditions. Even in the least favorably situated countries, however, there is much more potential capacity to carry out these studies than is commonly realized. It exists in university social science faculties and graduate student bodies, in underemployed returnees from overseas training, in medical and public health schools, in census and economic development agencies of government, and in the program staffs of health and family planning services. A political commitment to support this research with funds and leadership will attract more competent people from unexpected sources to do the work. In most cases only a few professional leaders, practical and program-oriented, are required to work out research priorities with program administrators, design the research methods, and monitor the work of a narrowly instructed staff. Some of the work can be contracted out, with an agreed research design, to universities and other institutions.

Useful action depends first of all on a personal commitment by the country's population program director to make research and operational evaluation central features of his program. The organizational system for setting research objectives and priorities, designing studies, training or instructing staff, contracting with outside individuals and institutions, and encouraging university research and training in demography and related fields may be inside the population administration or in a separate research and training center. It must, however, be oriented toward the operational questions facing the program manager. A separate center may be fully responsive to the needs of the program administrator and at the same time better able than he to induce other government agencies and educational institutions to participate in the research effort.

A prime function of a national social and operational research unit should be to get this work out of the cloisters and organize it in ways that will yield usable information. The state of the research art or methodology in social fields must be greatly improved. Here is an opportunity for high-quality technical assistance.

There are obvious advantages in linking research with training in a single institution or in several centers serving political subdivisions. But neither the research nor the training requirements of a population program should be fully provided by such centers. In order to assure maximum mobilization of national competence and fresh and objective insights, a deliberate effort should be made to involve universities, medical and public health schools, and other research or training institutions in both basic and operational research and in higher level training.

A national population research system must also be concerned with some aspects of contraceptive development and testing, particularly relating to effectiveness and users' reactions in normal conditions, continuation rates, side effects, and medical administrative problems. These are, in a sense, only medical facets of operational studies. They do not—and should not—remove the focus of a developing nation's population research from the social, behavioral, operational, and evaluative questions that can only be answered locally.

Developing countries with strong biomedical laboratory research capabilities ought to link this capacity to international contraceptive development projects rather than make it a competitor for management attention and funding in a national population research program. This is obviously preferable in the majority of developing countries that lack the technical resources to make a significant contribution to basic or applied contraceptive development. Individual scientists of the developing countries and some laboratories and clinical testing facilities can play important roles in international collaboration on specific contraceptive development schemes. Technical assistance can stimulate the development of biomedical expertise in developing countries. But there is little to be said in favor of the bureaucratic monstrosity sometimes suggested: a single comprehensive research and training center in each country dealing with biomedical and technological research, as well as social and operational research, plus training and evaluation.

International Collaboration

How can international cooperation make national population programs more effective? What better ways of engaging the professional and financial capacities of the developing countries and a concerned international community can be suggested for the decade ahead?

Population programs are rapidly outrunning the need for generalized foreign admonishment to "do something." This is not to say that political will is firmly established, even among governments that have accepted responsibility for doing something. But advocacy and prescriptions for change are more acceptable and effective when made by informed local citizens. Foreign technical assistance, therefore, ought to be used to strengthen the capacity of strategic local leaders, public or private, to analyze and act on population problems.

The pace and effectiveness of programs undertaken by the developing countries depend heavily on the competence, vigor, and quantity of local program staffs. Expatriate advisers can only marginally offset local inadequacies. Perpetuation of the manpower bottlenecks in population programs provides a justification for (as well as reflecting) weak political commitment and tokenism. Technical assistance, whether private, governmental, or multilateral, can help to reduce manpower problems.

Assistance should be devoted to establishing or strengthening training capabilities in universities, health institutions, and special centers designed to produce both professional and narrowly skilled manpower to carry out population programs. For the United States, at least, the most attractive means of providing this assistance is through long-term contracts, financed by the technical assistance agency, to enable U.S. university departments or population studies centers to put training specialists in local institutions of the developing countries. Long-term support, through endowed university "chairs" or some other means, should be given outstanding scholars of the developing countries who now lack freedom from teaching loads or necessary "moonlighting" to devote time to research, writing, or consultation services to national population programs.

Specific research and local training grants, preferably administered by local organizations, should be given to social and natural scientists, administrators, and others capable of contributing to better understanding of the problems and choices facing their national population programs. Developing country specialists and administrators should be given funds to participate in international professional seminars and observation tours to exchange knowledge in this new field. Teachers, advisers, and financial support should be provided to regional training centers serving groups of developing countries, when the regional approach offers advantages over national programs.

The success of population programs also depends on detailed knowledge of the demographic characteristics, forces, and trends in each country attempting to carry out a program. There are only limited possibilities for substituting international or regional research on behavioral and operational questions for the local study and experimental work each country must undertake. Substantial assistance should be devoted to the establishment of national programs of social and operational research and evaluation and to the provision of key professional staff to work in these national programs or centers. If local universities, other training institutions, and other governmental agencies are engaged in the effort, the opportunities for introducing foreign experts or teams to help carry out some of the studies and interpret their findings will be greatly enlarged.

Financial support of population program research, whether locally or jointly staffed, should be provided by assistance agencies to overcome traditional budgetary limits on research funding. If the efficiency of population programs and hence their prospects for expansion and broad impact are to increase, they must utilize the resources of health, education, and communications programs and of private enterprise.

The theoretical advantages of radical changes in a family planning delivery system or of exploiting other government and private programs to serve population programs are offset by many uncertainties about the wisdom of wholesale innovations, as well as by bureaucratic resistance. Pilot programs can introduce new methods without disrupting programs prematurely. Among examples of opportunities for technical assistance to pilot programs is the cooperative study by the Population Council and local institutions in fourteen countries comparing the costs and benefits of extending postpartum family planning services through all hospitals, or beyond hospitals to maternity clinics, with equal investment in extension of the program through other channels.

The Ghana Medical School and the School of Public Health

of the University of California at Los Angeles are testing methods of providing comprehensive family health services, including birth control, maternal and child health, nutrition and health education, using specially trained teams of doctors, sanitarians, midwives, community health nurses, and other personnel. Comparisons between different mixes of these components and a "control" community will shed some factual light on disputes over the best approaches to providing family planning services in combination with rural health, health education, and nutritional services. A multinational study similar to the Ghana experiment is being planned; using control and experimental populations in several countries, it will study the fertility consequences of combined population and general health services or population and maternal and child health services versus separately administered programs.

Western science and assistance organizations can take the leading role in solving the technological problems of population programs. Meeting the urgent need for a complete contraceptive technology adapted to local preferences and limitations is one of the most exciting challenges to international technical cooperation in the new decade. The effort will demand a sharp increase in public financing of basic and applied research, a systematic mobilization of scientists, laboratories, and testing facilities on an international scale, and a system of coordination and research management unprecedented in this field.

Multiple lines of inquiry must be pursued, allowing for exploration of blind alleys and test failures. Research-management units or programs must be added to the basic and applied studies when needed to assure followthrough to a usable product in the shortest possible time. Testing must be carried out simultaneously in several countries, including those less developed countries with good laboratory and clinical facilities, to minimize delays in acceptance of a new product.

New ways must be devised to combine public financing of research and the capacities of privately owned pharmaceutical industries. It is unlikely that the industry will finance development of contraceptives that require years of costly research and testing and have uncertain prospects of success or acceptance. The U.S. Center for Population Research has begun to offer contracts for NIH-financed research to the U.S. industry. Another approach might be to subsidize the costs of conducting long-term toxicity and clinical trials of products developed with private financing. In either case, the public subsidy probably must be conditioned on some surrender of proprietary rights to the product in licensing of commercial production.

Strong reserves of scientific capacity for research in this field exist in the universities and public research institutions of many countries. In a global survey, 145 institutions were found to have relevant research and training under way. About 35 ranked as "major" research units, with the full-time equivalent of at least two senior scientists and their coworkers. Seven ranked as "institutes," with five to ten senior investigators and a substantial supporting staff. All of the institutes and about half of the major and minor institutional efforts were in the United States, but Europe, Japan, Australia, Latin America, the Middle East, and developing countries of Asia and Africa were represented.[20]

A research effort equal to the challenge should fully engage this international scientific community and attract the requisite financial support of aid donors. At a minimum, a more cohesive network for exchanging information and discussing research strategy is essential. The WHO and the UN population program directors are in ideal positions to lead in this improvement in international coordination. The WHO practice of designating institutions specializing in particular subfields

20. Harkavy and Maier, "Research in Reproductive Biology and Contraceptive Technology."

of research as "international reference centers" responsible for promoting rapid exchange of research plans and findings would partially meet the needs.

Beyond this sort of international coordination, the next logical step is to build international research programs around the specialties of each of these designated "reference centers." Parts of these programs would be assigned to cooperating institutions so that many scientists could be employed at their home bases in both developed and less developed countries. Program directors would arrange for product testing by cooperating or contract institutions, including some in the countries most immediately interested in the new technology.

The alternative of a wholly new international research center with a staff of mixed nationality and links with national institutions has been suggested by the success of the international rice and wheat centers. It would meet the need for additional research-management capability and presumably could be more sharply product-oriented than the typical university-connected research laboratory or the fundamental research-oriented National Institutes of Health program. It would have very limited utility, however, if its management were not of top quality or it were located in a place where the best biomedical and biochemical researchers would not wish to live for several years with their families. Its international auspices also would have to be carefully arranged to insulate the center from the procedures and precedents of some international organizations. At best, such an international contraceptive-development center could be only one element of a network of research programs.

Summary

In the 1960s the world came to recognize the toll paid in frustrated aspirations and began to do something about runaway population growth in low-income countries. Contention about the population problem largely gave way to understanding of the interdependence of economic and social progress and restraint on human fertility. Population programs became a major new field of development, and pioneering countries began to demonstrate that the effort, though belated and difficult, could succeed. Their early experience also showed how much was yet to be learned and devised in order to make population programs effective everywhere.

The key requirements are a broad spectrum of safe and effective fertility-control techniques; systems for delivering services that can be expanded rapidly with slight dependence on professional medical personnel and at low cost; and means of extending and intensifying parental motivations to limit family size. All three depend upon a greater commitment of political and professional leadership, skills, and money to create and use better social and technological means. This is the classic problem-solving challenge to international technical cooperation. In the case of population programs, the urgency of the problem makes the opportunity doubly important.

Conventional, random action on the complex research and training tasks ahead would be totally inconsistent with the scale and urgency of needs. A more sharply focused system of research management, training, and program administration is a necessity. New arrangements are needed to facilitate professional collaboration between the institutions and program managers of the developing countries and growing pools of U.S. and other foreign specialists. The indispensable requirement is active involvement of the best social and biological scientists, the pharmaceutical industry, training institutions, and administrative experts.

Private U.S. initiatives, increasingly supported by public funds, made crucial contributions to the pioneering efforts to check excessive birthrates. An expanding U.S. official commitment to population program assistance would add little if it discouraged further enlargement of private American participation. The programs of the U.S. technical assistance agency and the National Institutes of Health should be designed to evoke larger and more diverse involvement by professional communities. Essential to this goal are an assurance of long-term contracts and grants by governmental agencies and a sense of responsibility for initiating collaborative arrangements on the part of the private institutions.

All concerned must somehow maintain a sense of urgency for a very long haul.

CHAPTER SIX

Nutrition's Emerging Role in National Development

"ALTHOUGH the concern of Governments in improved nutrition is by no means new, action has in the past generally been limited in scope. . . . Millions of people in all parts of the globe are either suffering from inadequate physical development or from diseases due to malnutrition or are living in a state of sub-normal health which could be improved if they consumed more or different food. . . . [This] situation . . . remains an outstanding challenge to constructive statesmanship and international cooperation.

"The movement towards better nutrition in the past has been largely the result of the unconscious and instinctive groping of men for a better and more abundant life. What is now required is the conscious direction of the natural tendency towards better nutrition. Such direction constitutes policy. . . . For nutrition policy to be effective, the problem must be recognized as one of primary national importance."[1]

That admonition, still pertinent, was made in a League of Nations report in 1937. Thirty years later the United Nations attempted to rally international action to deal seriously with malnutrition:

Today there are over 300 million children who, for lack of sufficient protein and calories, suffer grossly retarded physical growth

1. *Final Report of the Mixed Committee of the League of Nations on The Relation of Nutrition to Health, Agriculture and Economic Policy* (Geneva: League of Nations, 1937).

and development, and for many of these mental development, learning and behavior may be impaired as well. Protein-calorie deficiencies also directly affect the health and economic productivity of adult populations. Such nutritional deficits, damaging both present and future generations are built-in handicaps which must be corrected.

It is now recognized that the protein problem is reaching a critical stage. It is essential that the United Nations family urgently take action aimed at closing the present gap between world protein needs and protein supplies and at preventing even more widespread protein deficiency in future generations.[2]

These and other warnings have challenged development planners to stop treating nutrition, especially among young children, as simply a welfare or consumption factor. If the case has not been overdrawn, malnutrition is a prime cause, not just a symptom, of self-perpetuating poverty. It compounds the burden of infectious disease, stunts and limits the learning capacity of millions of children, saps the efficiency of workers, and stifles creativity and ambition. In sum, protein–calorie malnutrition, and to a lesser degree other nutritional deficiencies, are an insidious brake on economic development as well as a monstrous social injustice.

Yet nutrition has remained at the margins of development thinking. Its case has been poorly represented. In nearly all governments, nutrition has no power base. It is typically the concern of welfare services, usually expressed in child-feeding gestures, piecemeal efforts to inform or educate on nutritional principles, and superficial clinical treatment of maternal and child health problems stemming from malnutrition. It is part of the baggage of the educational and health systems and agricultural extension, community development, and other agencies, but in most countries nutrition is not a principal concern

2. UN, Advisory Committee on the Application of Science and Technology, "International Action to Avert the Impending Protein Crisis" (a report to the Economic and Social Council, 1968; processed).

of any institution that is powerful in determining development policy. Nutritional improvement is an assumed benefit of economic growth, but it rarely if ever is a decisive consideration in the making of agricultural or general economic policy. Foreign economic assistance agencies seldom stress nutritional objectives or country development efforts on nutrition in judging competing claims for their funds.

The UN World Health Organization (WHO), Food and Agriculture Organization (FAO), and Children's Emergency Fund (UNICEF) have jointly sought for nearly a decade to promote pilot "applied nutrition" projects. Many governments have set up the national interministerial coordinating committees that the UN agencies require in their assistance arrangement to awaken concern and spur governmental action on nutritional problems. In all but a few countries, however, these committees and the pilot projects they coordinate have lacked the resources and drive to rise above token approaches to nutrition problems.

Malnutrition is a complex social affliction whose cure requires treating many interacting elements of a society. Like other multisectoral problems, it tends to fall between the bureaucratic stools when it is approached with "coordination" instead of leadership at the level of political policy making and overall development strategy.

The Future of Nutrition Programs

If nutrition should remain at the fringes of development programs in the 1970s, Development Decade II would fall needlessly short of its goals in raising the "quality of life" of the poor. There are some encouraging signs that this may not be the prospect—that nutrition is beginning to move into greater prominence on development policy agendas. New knowledge and techniques have made direct attacks on the major dietary deficiencies of the less developed countries appear more manageable and more promising.

The specter of approaching famine, which in many countries forced concern in agricultural production to concentrate almost exclusively on increasing quantity, has given way to a greater confidence in their ability to meet total food demand, at least in this decade. Now it is possible to turn attention to the breeding of staple crops to raise protein quality and usable quantity; to meat, milk, and fisheries production; and to pricing and distribution policies benefiting the low-income producer and consumer. The high-yielding cereal varieties are raising land productivity and giving countries that can use them the option of increasing cereal output at lower prices. They also are making possible diversification to crops high in nutritional quality or to export crops that help finance imports of protective foods. Nutritional considerations now have an opportunity to figure prominently in agricultural policy making, research, and training.

So long as government leaders equated all nutritional deficiencies with poverty, their conception of nutrition policy seemed to be limited to a slow, general increase in incomes and food supplies, coupled with token efforts to feed the most needy. Since the mid-1960s a growing body of widely publicized medical, food science, and social science findings has given policy makers a chance to see that their countries' nutrition problems are divisible and subject to more discrete treatment.

Research has identified the principal targets for nutrition policy as weanling infants, preschool children, and pregnant or nursing mothers in all poor communities. These vulnerable groups are also the main targets of national health services, of combined health and population services, and of local community welfare programs. Nutritional prevention, rescue, and education efforts can be extended along with these services throughout a country at a low additional administrative cost. The integration of family planning with nutrition and maternal and child health programs may be the best long-term approach to all three objectives.

Research on food values in human metabolism also has revealed that the task of correcting the most serious dietary deficiencies of older children and adults (other than pregnant and nursing women) in the cereal-eating countries is not so overwhelming as estimates that stressed animal protein gaps had implied. For these groups malnutrition often is a simple calorie shortage, whose solution lies mainly in economic development, especially among subsistence-farming villagers. Where people can afford enough calories, local cereals, beans, peas, and other garden vegetables can provide a low-cost means of reaching nearly adequate levels of protein–mineral nutrition for the majority of adults and older children. The variety of potential means of closing nutritional gaps in urban diets is increasing as basic foods are fortified and new protective foods formulated at relatively low cost.

Research also is producing evidence, still not conclusive at the beginning of the 1970s, that protein–calorie malnutrition before birth and in the first several years of life can permanently limit brain development.[3] The incidence of retardation

3. P. Rosso, J. Hormazabal, and M. Winick, "Changes in Brain Weight, Cholesterol, Phospholipid and DNA Content in Marasmic Children," *American Journal of Clinical Nutrition*, Vol. 23, No. 10 (1970); M. Winick, "Brain Development during Malnutrition" (paper presented to Pan American Health Organization [PAHO] Advisory Committee on Medical Research, June 1968); E. Botha-Antoun, S. Babayan, and J. K. Harfouche, "Intellectual Development Related to Nutritional Status," *Journal of Tropical Pediatrics* (Kingston, Jamaica), September 1968; Alan D. Berg, "Malnutrition and National Development," *Journal of Tropical Pediatrics*, September 1968; R. F. Frisch, "Malnutrition and Mental Retardation," *American Journal of Clinical Nutrition*, Vol. 23, No. 2 (1970).

due to malnutrition and whether it is irreversible are not known. However, even if it is found that much or all of the retardation can be corrected by belated dietary balance and clinical rehabilitation, will these children of the most impoverished circumstances be rescued in fact, and in time? And will they be able to make up for the lost opportunities for learning and psychological and physical development in the critical early years?

There is little debate about the other human costs of protein–calorie malnutrition in infants and small children. In varying degrees it is believed to afflict over one-third of all children below age five in the less developed countries (see Table 6-1).

TABLE 6-1. *Estimated Incidence of Protein–Calorie Malnutrition in Children, Selected Countries,* 1969[a]

In percent

	Children under 5 years with protein–calorie malnutrition			Children under 5 years that die before fifth birthday
Country	Severe[b]	Moderate[c]	Total	
India	1.4–2.9	16.0	17.4–18.9	28.1
Uganda	4.9	27.2	32.1	n.a.
Malawi	3.2	25.8	29.0	n.a.
Guatemala	4.1	24.5	28.6	18.5
Chile	2.6	32.0	34.6	12.6
Mexico				
Urban areas	1.3	14.8	16.1	n.a.
Rural areas	3.4	27.5	30.9	n.a.
United States[d]	n.a.	n.a.	n.a.	2.5

Source: A. D. Berg and A. Watkins, "Recent Trends on Prevalence of P-CM" (paper prepared for Protein Advisory Group, FAO/WHO/UNICEF, September 1969).

n.a.: Not available.

a. Figures for Uganda, Guatemala, and Chile are for 1967.

b. Body growth 60 percent or less of norm for age and population group.

c. Body growth 61–79 percent of norm for age and population group.

d. Fragmentary clinical evidence indicates that protein deficiencies are not pronounced in diets of low-income U.S. children.

It is the greatest single cause, direct and indirect, of the staggering death rates and repetitive illness among children in these countries. It usually kills by increasing vulnerability to enteric and respiratory infections and otherwise routine childhood diseases. Repeated infections and fever further deplete body reserves of protein. Poor absorption of nutrients through the chronically infected intestinal tracts seems to cause secondary malnutrition. It is largely for these interacting reasons that death rates in the one through four age group in the less developed countries range from five to fifteen times those of the developed countries. The chances of a child's reaching age six in many poor countries are no better than a North American's reaching age sixty. Those who survive are likely to be physically stunted. If their malnutrition persists into school age, they may never fully overcome their early physical handicaps and are likely to be apathetic, slow learners.

Figure 6-1 shows the provisional findings of studies of childhood mortality in eight Latin American urban and adjacent rural areas. Considerably higher childhood death rates prevail in less urbanized areas of Latin America and in lower income countries of Asia and Africa.

Adults, as well as children, suffer the consequences of other preventable deficiencies in diets. Most widespread are complex nutritional anemias, vitamin A deficiency (which can cause blindness), and iodine deficiency (which causes millions of cases of goiter and sometimes permanent damage to the nervous system).[4]

National Nutrition Programs

This evolving knowledge of nutrition and the means of attacking particular deficiencies has begun to stimulate public

4. Nevin S. Scrimshaw, "Worldwide Opportunities for Food Scientists and Technologists," *Food Technology*, Vol. 17, No. 7 (1963), and

FIGURE 6-1. *Deaths of Children under Five Years of Age Associated with Nutritional Deficiency, Thirteen Latin American Cities, 1968–69*[a]

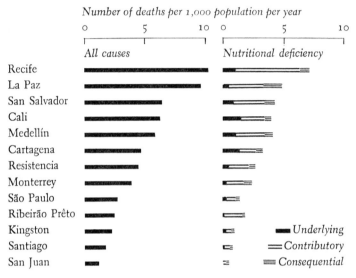

Source: Pan American Health Organization, *Inter-American Investigation of Mortality in Childhood* (Washington: PAHO, 1971), p. 49.
a. Excludes deaths at birth.

action that can be regarded as national policies and programs. Colombia, India, and Tunisia are among the pioneers in this movement, and other countries are adding nutrition legislation and programs without formally consolidating national policies. The ways in which this is happening suggest some useful roles for research and international technical cooperation.

"Food: World Problems," in the *International Encyclopedia of the Social Sciences* (Macmillan Company and Free Press, 1968).

Colombia's Institute System

Colombia began by taking seriously the WHO/FAO/ UNICEF proposals that applied nutrition programs be established and expanded as multisectoral development efforts. The government recognized that it needed an administrative structure to bring all the independent interests together in a common cause. In late 1962 it established the National Institute of Nutrition, gave it a continuing share of the income from sale of iodized salt by a government monopoly, and put the institute under a board of directors including the ministers of public health, education, and agriculture, and the director of the Association of Medical Schools. A physician specializing in public health nutrition was made director. The institute's four divisions were given coordinating—and to a substantial degree directive—authority over Colombia's applied nutrition program, supplementary feeding services, nutrition education, and nutrition research. In May 1969 the institute became the Direction of Nutrition of the Colombian Institute for Family Welfare, a new agency responsible for all aspects of assistance to underprivileged mothers and children.

The institute's first director set it on a course of integrating analysis, research, planning, training, and operations.[5] Most public-service programs continued to be carried on by the health, education, agriculture, and community development institutions, including the established Pronenca program of direct feeding and nutrition education serving about 2 million mothers and children. The institute provided the analysis and diagnosis of nutritional needs and techniques to guide these programs and trained some of their key staff at university and

5. R. Rueda-Williamson, "The Applied Nutrition Program, the Basis of the National Nutrition Plan," *PAHO Bulletin*, Vol. 68, No. 3 (Washington, 1970).

intermediate levels. It developed with general educational institutions new curricula for teaching nutrition in medical schools and created a school for nutritionist-dieticians oriented to public health service. It set up an ambitious "multiplier" scheme for training some 100,000 potentially available teachers, nursing auxiliaries, agricultural extension workers, home economics advisers, community development promoters, physicians, dentists, registered nurses, and volunteers. In the first six years, about 30,000 of these mostly part-time nutrition program workers were trained.

The institute and its successor organization set nutrition standards, prepared legislative and regulatory recommendations, and designed programs for decision and action by the development planning office of the presidency and the ministries concerned. It has provided technical advice to both planning and operating agencies. It evaluates all nutrition programs and carries on applied research.

Its major research efforts include:

Acceptability tests and demand for new protein-rich foods, determination of the iodide content of salt entering consumer markets, establishment of Colombian growth standards for children, nutritional composition of various foods produced in the country and of locally prepared dishes, preparation of food balance sheets, recommendations pertaining to consumption and target availabilities of food for the next 10 years, simplification of nutritional surveys, treatment of tropical anemia, the problems of absorption and intestinal parasites, the enrichment of weaning foods, the relationship beween malnutrition and mental development, use of opaque-2 corn for human consumption, and methodological research in various nutritional services and activities, such as the teaching of basic concepts of nutrition in elementary schools and the organization and operation of nutrition education and recuperation services.[6]

The institute's professional staff had grown from 22 in 1963

6. Ibid.

to 187 in 1970. Its budget had risen from about $200,000 the first year to about $4 million in 1970 (20 cents per capita), exclusive of support from the World Food Program, U.S. food aid, and voluntary agencies.

Colombia's strong start in making nutrition an important element of national development strategy began with a small group of Colombian public health doctors who were able to convince government leaders of the impact of nutritional problems on social and economic progress. Once such an activist group has achieved some official encouragement and an institutional base, they "should be given significant technical and economic assistance with a view to expanding and strengthening the supervisory technical team and promoting ever greater interest in nutrition programs in government circles. In each country such assistance will stimulate the allocation of more substantial resources—both technical and economic—for nutrition programs at a high priority level within government plans for accelerated social and economic development."[7]

India Pioneers

India has made the most formal and comprehensive commitment to the struggle against malnutrition. With the adoption of an extensive nutrition program in its current (1969–74) Five Year Plan, the Indian government launched a concerted effort to mobilize thousands of central and local government units, community organizations, training and research institutions, private industry, and international assistance agencies to reduce that vast country's more critical nutrition problems. A member of the Indian Planning Commission chairs the Nutrition Coodinating Committee which monitors assigned action of each participating agency.

7. Ibid.

India's recognition of nutrition as an important factor in national development preceded its independence. It was one of the first countries to set up a national nutrition committee in response to the 1937 League of Nations recommendations. The founders of independent India provided in the constitution that "the State shall regard the raising of the level of nutrition and the standards of living of its people and the improvement of public health as among its primary duties." Early development plans suggested measures to deal with malnutrition but did not translate them into directives or budgets binding government agencies. There was, however, a continual strengthening of nutrition units in several government agencies, especially the research capabilities of institutions concerned with agriculture, health, and food science and technology. These evolutionary steps, coupled with professional training, built a base of unusual competence for later action.

The transition from concern—expressed in policy documents and piecemeal feeding programs—to concerted action was accelerated by Prime Minister Indira Gandhi. Her wing of the ruling Congress Party moved ahead of her government in advocating a "children's charter" to guarantee a minimum diet to 80 million preschool children. Political commitment at the top has encouraged bold initiatives by subordinates. A number of other factors have been important also.

A major famine in Bihar state, breakthroughs in food technology, organized initiatives by the private food industry, and pressures by newspaper editors, scientists, and senior civil servants combined to enhance the government's willingness to experiment with new approaches. Actions on the new opportunities, although individually marginal, created a sense of momentum, exciting wide interest and optimism. Policy makers were stimulated to take more determined action by evidence that the great majority of Indian children suffered from "malnutritional dwarfism," provoking fears that "India could be raising a generation of substandard citizens."[8] Development planners faced up to the harsh arithmetic of the nutrition problem: even at good, sustained rates of economic growth, it would take more than a generation to raise the lowest one-third of India's incomes enough to afford adequate diets, assuming present food choices and price relationships.

The technological horizon was extended by the introduction of protein-rich combination flours in the child-feeding programs supported by the United States and by local production of "balahar." Balahar is a children's food combining donated U.S. whole wheat flour with Indian peanut flour, skim milk, vitamins, and minerals. India's first large-scale experiment with a ready-to-eat enriched food was the introduction in 1968 of "modern bread," produced by nine government plants. As production moved toward the initial goal of 100 million loaves a year, the market was found to include surprisingly low-income levels in the cities and nearby rural areas.

Modern bread and balahar led the way to adoption of a general policy favoring fortification of staples and a series of projects designed to reach low-income diets by this route. First was the fortification with vitamins, minerals, and peanut flour of the ground wheat "atta," which is used in making the bread-like "chapatti," a staple of northern India's diets. Again, however, the market will be largely urban—a not inconsequential 100 million people, but not the rural masses who do their own milling or depend upon small village mills. Searching for ways to reach some of the latter population, including small children, the Indians turned to experimental fortification of tea

8. Alan D. Berg, "Nutrition as a National Priority: Lessons from the India Experiment," *American Journal of Clinical Nutrition*, Vol. 23, No. 11 (1970), and "Priority of Nutrition in National Development," *Nutrition Reviews*, August 1970.

and salt and a further search for practical ways of fortifying rice and other whole grains at the village mill without loss of the enriching materials during cooking.

Private food and pharmaceutical companies, collaborating with public laboratories and agencies through a new Protein Foods Association of India, put more than two dozen new, nutritious food products into development and market-testing in a period of just over two years.[9] The industry group has undertaken a leading role in nutrition education with a movie, radio, and publication campaign keyed to a simple theme: "Your child's plate is his horoscope." Commercial advertising firms and market research also are being used to sharpen the targeting of the government's public education campaign.

The diversity of approaches and participants in India's expanding nutrition programs is suggested by a listing of nutrition projects—some of which may remain largely on paper—in the Five Year Plan. The Department of Health list included "feasible test of vitamin and mineral fortification of staple foods" (at the Central Food Technological Research Institute and 3 other research centers); "pilot project on nutrition education through State Nutrition Bureaus" (involving 6 state governments and using mobile van units); "establishment and strengthening of nutrition divisions in states"; "training of hospital dieticians" (45 at 10 centers). The Department of Family Planning was to conduct "prophylaxis against nutrition anemia in mothers and children" (15 million beneficiaries) and "program for control of blindness in children caused by vitamin A deficiency" (16 million children under five). The Department of Community Development planned "applied nutrition program" (community level promotion of noncereal agricultural production and related nutrition education) and "composite program for women and pre-school children" (through village level women's volunteer organizations).

9. Berg, "Nutrition as a National Priority."

The Department of Food list included "production of groundnut flour"; "production of balahar"; "production of weaning foods" (including market studies and promotion); assistance to dairies in production of "protein isolate toned milk"; "pilot plant for protein isolate production"; "production of cottonseed flour for human consumption" (provision of equipment to private millers and quality control inspection); "establishment of techniques of production of fortified wheat products"; "fortification of salt"; "fortification of bread" (promotion of fortification by private bakers) and "mobile food and nutrition extension units." The Ministry of Education planned a "school feeding program" (with coverage targets rising from 11 million children in 1969 to 15 million in 1973). The Department of Social Welfare anticipated preschool feeding of needy children through over 6,000 local welfare offices.

Outside the nutrition chapter of the Five Year Plan are other large-scale government programs, particularly in agriculture, that contribute to the nutrition effort. Agricultural research and production agencies are working on improving or simplifying the processing of soybeans and cottonseed, the introduction of more efficient techniques for extracting vegetable oil, the reduction of waste in processing and storage of food crops, adjustment of farm production toward higher protein foods, and genetic improvement of cereals and pulses. A multiyear campaign called Operation Flood aims to improve the quantity and quality of urban milk supplies.

Tunisia's Program

Tunisia is at the early stages of establishing a comprehensive nutrition program. Like Colombia, Tunisia began with a revealing study of its nutritional diseases and some crude estimates of their impact on the health and economic productivity of the people. This study by a government committee influenced the strategy of Tunisia's Four Year Plan for 1969–72 and led to a presidential decision to consolidate food and nutrition activities in a National Institute of Nutrition and Food Technology.

The Tunisian institute is to build from an initially small staff the capacity to design, coordinate, and direct nutrition programs and to recommend policy and legislation. Its director is appointed by the president of Tunisia on the nomination of the health minister. He is assisted by a "technical committee" including representatives of the Ministries of Education, Agriculture, and National Economy and various consumers' organizations.

The institute's duties are to establish locally valid nutritional standards; carry out nutritional surveys; provide technical guidance to the school and institutional feeding programs; develop (with foreign agencies) weaning and children's foods based on Tunisian products; foster improvements in commercial and home processing and preservation of foods; develop nutritious foods for the low-income markets; train nutrition teachers and trainers; devise better nutrition teaching aids; design, technically supervise, and evaluate nutrition training and education; undertake economic studies of food consumption and distribution; analyze alternative methods of providing nutrition services; make marketing surveys for new or improved foods; and recommend economic policies affecting food production and nutrition. To fulfill these large expectations, the institute will need to supplement its limited staff with individual foreign specialists and teams while seeking to recruit and train Tunisians.

The institute's first major activity—actually begun before the institute was in operation—has been the sponsorship of a four-year experimental project on fortification of wheat flour. This project, in cooperation with the Harvard University School of

Public Health, is one of four large-scale studies initiated and supported by the Agency for International Development on the technology, economics, marketing, and human vitality consequences of multiple fortification of staple foods.[10]

Nutrition Strategy

A serious attack on nutrition problems demands policy and program decisions cutting across virtually every development sector. The ultimate goals of a national nutrition policy are likely to be almost as broad as "success" in comprehensive economic and social development: average incomes for the poorest stratum of the population high enough to pay for adequate diets, popular understanding of how to achieve an adequate diet at lowest cost, control of diseases that severely drain the body of nutrients or cause malabsorption of nutrients, and a food supply adequate to meet dietary needs. Merely stating these long-term goals reveals the necessity of targeting intermediate and attainable objectives.

Nutrition policy, like health policy, should serve to accelerate overall development rather than passively depend on economic growth, more equitable income distribution, health, and educational services to solve nutrition problems. Waiting for nutritional needs to be solved by economic growth means forgoing opportunities over the next ten to thirty years for faster and more equitable progress. Hoping for rising incomes to be translated eventually into better diets is to ignore the fact that lack of knowledge of proper diet—particularly on the part of mothers—is a prominent cause of the malnutrition–infection synergism in millions of homes today. Increased income

10. Interview with Martin Forman, Office of Nutrition, AID, 1971. The other projects deal with fortification of rice in Thailand, of corn meal in Guatemala, and of manioc (cassava) in Brazil.

may cause shifts to "higher status" but not necessarily more nutritious foods—from pounded to polished rice, unrefined to refined sugar, yellow corn to less nutritious white bread, tea and biscuits instead of curd and chapatti, and so on.[11]

Counting on increased agricultural production or even balanced food supplies alone to take care of nutritional deficiencies also is a delusion. Unless governments take strong action to intervene in the processes, rising and more diversified agricultural production may be accompanied by increasing disparities in income or no reduction in the relative prices of protective foods, thus failing to benefit the lowest income groups most commonly suffering from malnutrition.

The procedural steps in organizing national nutrition programs are likely to be critical in getting the right forces mobilized and coordinated from the start. Before and after the organizational decisions, however, come tougher questions of exactly how the country is to make nutrition and other development forces mutually reinforcing. Should the policy concentrate on directly serving selected target groups or aim to serve the entire population through more indirect means? Assuming it should be at least partially selective, should its prime target be the most nutritionally vulnerable (the infants, preschool children, and frequently pregnant mothers in the poorest families) or those most able to contribute to economic productivity (the older children and workers)?

Can the delivery of dietary supplements to the selected target groups through welfare, health, and school systems be financed and managed without sacrificing other important goals of national development? What delivery system can reach preschool children and infants most efficiently or with greatest benefit to other social development objectives? What

11. Alan D. Berg, "Increased Income and Improved Nutrition: A Shibboleth Examined," *International Development Review*, Fall 1970.

combination of educational and incentive measures can effectively change their mothers' feeding practices?

Apart from administrative feasibility and cost, is the provision of daily government rations to a large fraction of the country's population good public policy? Or would general improvement of the nutritional quality of staple foods through fortification be more socially healthful and administratively sensible, even if it missed large numbers of rural poor? Should the program forgo attempting to reach rural families in favor of more complete service to the rapidly growing concentrations of urban poor?

How and at what price should agricultural production or diversification and marketing be adjusted to serve nutritional needs of the low-income groups? Should agricultural policy aim at boosting incomes of small farmers if this conflicts with the objective of maximizing food production and holding down prices for the urban poor? Should the government subsidize the production and marketing of highly nutritious foods at low prices? To what degree can this use of the marketing system substitute for direct feeding, education, or health programs? Should the policy rely on promoting balanced diets through diversified selection of natural foods, or must it also seek to make traditional food staples as nutritionally complete as possible through mandatory fortification at processing plants? At what cost and risk of poor quality controls? Should improvements in the quality and coverage of public health services be concentrated on maternal and child care so as to complement nutritional and family planning programs?

These are questions for the nation's central development policy makers and political leaders. Poor answers will waste critical resources and cripple other programs. Good answers depend on balancing the knowledge and judgment of specialists in food science, food technology, health, agriculture, education, public administration, and the social sciences.

Unhappily, this expert knowledge is likely to be composed more of parochial enthusiasms than of hard facts for economic analysis and program selection. Few countries know—beyond crude estimates drawn from income-based food-basket surveys and sampling—the particular nutritional deficiencies of their population groups, by age, geographic area, occupation, or income. While there are impressive examples of measured increases in productivity of workers and students attributed to dietary improvements, experts differ on how much of this can be credited to increases in calories (that is, quantity) and how much to protein or other qualitative (for example, iron) enrichment of their diets. The extent, permanence, and developmental significance of mental and physical retardation caused by protein–calorie deficiencies in diets of infants and preschool children is unclear and unquantified. Even the oldest large-scale nutrition activities, school feeding and food-for-work projects, have not produced acceptable records of resultant performance gains. The cost-effectiveness of alternative systems for providing nutrition services has not been tested systematically. Few of the promising opportunities offered by the new food technology have been marketed long enough to reveal their actual potential for closing nutritional gaps in the lowest income and most vulnerable elements of the population.

In short, the quantitative effects of nutrition program actions on improved nutrition and on labor productivity have not been fully enough demonstrated to serve as a guide in program budgeting. This does not argue for doing nothing until more complete survey findings or other research results are in hand. (No further nutritional studies are needed to demonstrate the benefits of agricultural policies encouraging greater production of beans and peas, for example.) It does, however, suggest that most elements of a nutrition program should be planned, managed, and evaluated as large-scale experiments. The experimental approach can yield more useful information than studies that do not accompany action attempting to change a situation.[12]

Improving Basic Food Supplies

In most developing countries a nutrition strategy must work on both the market supply and the market demand for food in addition to more direct or selective measures for combating food problems. Most countries know their aggregate food supplies and nutrient requirements well enough to project approximate demand for major sources of calories and proteins with rough accuracy some distance into the future. They do not know enough about their protein shortages, in terms of either optimum or effective demand, to determine their decisions on agricultural policy. But it is clear that the higher price of proteins, along with ignorance, tradition, and taboos, concentrates the scarcity among those who need proteins most—the very young, the self-sacrificing mother, and the destitute sick. Where there are calorie shortages as well (the usual case), the protein deficiency is compounded because the body tends to use proteins for energy, leaving less for building tissues and as reserves against the nitrogen drain of disease and increased needs of pregnancy or lactation.

A nutrition strategy must, therefore, assure that the *quantity* of available calories keeps pace with real demand (including institutional feeding and other government efforts to increase food demand), so that the price rationing of scarcity will not penalize the poor. The strategy also must address the *quality* of the basic food supply, particularly the prices and variety of protein sources.

Agricultural supply policy can include a combination of

12. Interview with Aaron Altschul, 1970.

means aimed at increasing total agricultural production and reducing losses in the field, in storage, and in processing and cooking; increasing the protein content and quality of basic foods such as cereals through plant breeding and increasing the quantity of protein-rich staples such as beans; and increasing production of meat, dairy products, and fish where this can be done efficiently. (In most low-income countries, government encouragement of meat production amounts to a subsidy for the small minority of upper-income meat buyers.)

Boosting Demand for Protective Foods

The second major facet of a nutrition strategy is the conversion of nutritional need into effective market demand. This cannot be left to the slow processes of general economic and social development. More discriminating measures acting on the demand side can be tried, such as: production and marketing subsidies for fortified or specially formulated foods; official credit and other production supports and price-stabilization measures designed to keep conventional foods (basic calorie sources as well as proteins) within the reach of low-income buyers; government-guaranteed markets to encourage private production of enriched food formulations; and government-financed testing, market development, and public education promoting the use of protective foods by low-income buyers. These can be costly and speculative interventions in the market. (For example, an attempt to control urban food prices may weaken production incentives or defeat other measures to hold redundant population in rural areas.) Such interventions should be treated as experiments, with results evaluated frequently.

Agricultural and fisheries production and marketing approaches will help, but they are unlikely to provide much relief for the prime victims of malnutrition, the lowest income and least educated mothers, infants, and young children. Nutrition strategy must, therefore, look to the potential role of food technology in indirect or marketing approaches to problems. Technology offers a pair of new dimensions in new food formulations and staple food fortification.

New Foods

Laboratory food science and technology have far outpaced knowledge of the social or real-life effects of food modification schemes that are widely used. The FAO and WHO, especially, have extended broadly the understanding of nutritional values of common foods, individually and combined. The once obscure distinctions between protein quality and quantity, as determined by the amino acid profiles of natural food proteins, have become familiar ground to laymen. While experts continue to debate means of measurement, it is possible to gauge the approximate nutritive values of combinations of proteins from such sources as peanuts, beans, chickpeas, grain bran and other milling byproducts, rice, wheat flour, milk solids, or fish flour in both intermediate and complete food products. The cost of a unit of usable protein in combined food products can now be calculated with rough accuracy although the exercise is misleading if the other components of an individual's total diet are unknown.

Food industries and public food technology laboratories are creating protein-rich combined flours, weaning foods, beverages, bread, and other ready-to-eat products aimed at middle and lower middle income markets and institutional feeding programs. As marketing instruments in national nutrition programs, the new foods can make only a limited contribution on a dependable, daily basis to correcting nutritional deficiencies of the lowest income groups that are in greatest need. (They do make public feeding programs more effective and attractive and help the cause of popular education in nutrition.) None of the new foods had significantly penetrated the lowest income markets of predominantly rural countries by the end of the 1960s. To establish a solid place in those markets, a new food must be little if any more expensive than the traditional food it replaces. Its appeal will depend more on taste and on ease and familiarity of household use than on nutritional quality.

In countries with large lower middle income groups in urbanized areas, new food formulations can increase the variety of dietary choices and improve some marginal diets. This seems to be the prospect for Vita-Soy in Hong Kong, enriched atta and bread in the cities of India, Incaparina products in urban areas of Central and South America, and Pro-Nutro products in South Africa.

Fortification

Food technology's greatest contribution to national nutrition programs probably lies in fortification of familiar primary foods. The addition at processing points of tasteless, odorless protein, mineral, and vitamin additives to wheat flour, corn meal, rice, cassava, or tea by means that require no change in food habits and little added burden to the lowest income food budgets seems to offer great advantages. It is independent of the slow and uneven process of nutrition education. It seems capable of reaching some village wage-earners as well as all urban dwellers, weaning as well as older children and adults. Fortification is of little use, however, in correcting protein–calorie malnutrition among traditional subsistence-farming families, small infants, or those poor and sick children who do not get or cannot digest sufficient total calories.

Fortification of foods distributed through market channels has established its effectiveness and simplicity in dealing with several deficiency diseases other than protein–calorie malnutrition. Iodization of salt is a well-established means of controlling goiter and associated diseases at very low cost. Central American countries, as well as developed countries, have for many years enriched wheat flour and corn meal with thiamine, riboflavin, and niacin to prevent beriberi and pellagra. Fortification seems to be a simple means of correcting vitamin A and calcium deficiency diseases without great cost or effect on the cooking and eating qualities of the carrier food.

Protein-enrichment of diets through large-scale and long-term fortification is yet to be proved effective. Four major operational research projects supported by AID have begun comprehensive tests on wheat flour, corn meal, rice, and cassava (manioc) fortification in four countries. India has gone into a large-scale experiment in fortification of atta flour and is studying lysine, iron, and calcium fortification of salt and tea. Laboratory evidence is promising, but many biological, technical, and financial questions remain to be answered. Among these are: Does amino acid fortification increase protein utilization significantly in the varied and variable real-life diets of these countries, particularly those of the youngest children in low-income families, where total calorie supply may be the limiting factor? Will the fortified foodstuffs actually be allocated to the youngsters within the family in sufficient quantity to correct their malnutrition?

Protein fortification should be aimed at compensating for limitations in the amino acid balance of the target population's "normal" diet, not simply the limitations in the carrier staple food. However, without much more knowledge than usually is available on the micro-nutrient composition of total diets, a compromise approximation will have to be struck on the type and quantity of protein additives to be used in a large-scale and standardized fortification program.

Synthetic amino acids or protein concentrates derived from

natural protein sources such as soy beans, cottonseed, peanuts, fish, skim milk, or egg may be used. Both kinds of additives raise the limiting amino acids in the carrier staple such as wheat flour and in the presumed total diet of the consumer. The concentrates also provide a small increase in the quantity of protein and other nutrients in the diet. Amino acid fortification has the advantage of requiring only minute quantities of the additive, easing the logistic problem. For example, the addition of 0.2 percent lysine to wheat flour raises the usable protein from about 3.2 percent of the total weight of flour to about 5.3 percent; the addition of 0.3 percent lysine and 0.1 percent threonine to rice increases its proportion of usable protein from 4.5 percent to 7.5 percent.[13] The use of a natural concentrate in fortification allows a somewhat greater margin for error in knowledge of the amino acid composition of total diets among the target population than does the use of a single synthetic amino acid. On the other hand, some of the natural concentrates have undesirable effects on the taste or other characteristics of the fortified food.

Prices of lysine and natural protein concentrates are about the same. Synthetic tryptophan (used in corn meal fortification) and threonine (used in rice fortification) were considerably more expensive than lysine in 1970; but their prices were expected to decline if demand grew enough to justify mass production or technological innovation.

The cost of fortifying wheat flour in Tunisia with lysine, vitamins, and minerals has been estimated at about $5.50 per ton of flour, or about $1.10 per capita per year. Slightly lower costs have been estimated for wheat flour fortification in

13. D. M. Hegsted, "Nutritional Value of Cereal Proteins in Relation to Human Needs," in Max Milner (ed.), *Protein-Enriched Cereal Foods for World Needs* (St. Paul, Minn.: American Association of Cereal Chemists, 1969), and findings quoted by Altschul in private interview, 1970.

Pakistan.[14] Rice fortification will cost somewhat more—but about the same percentage of the basic grain price—because it presents more complex technical problems. The most promising technique seems to be the addition at each rice mill of a small proportion of rice-like grains carrying the fortifying ingredients in a casing that resists rapid dissolution in cooking water. This process will add at least 5 percent to the rice price; government subsidies would entail considerable administrative difficulty as well as cost. Selective subsidies protecting only the lowest income consumers of fortified products would be virtually impossible to administer and police. One of the questions to be answered in pilot fortification projects is whether the poor will eat less, substantially defeating the nutrition program's purpose, to offset a price increase on their staple cereal of 4–6 percent.

Fortification of carbohydrate foods as part of a marketing approach to nutrition is least promising where the needy population is predominantly rural and its prime source of calories is a carbohydrate food milled at home or in many small mills beyond the effective reach of government directives or government logistic and financial support. In these cases an alternative carrier of the enrichment ingredients might be a common-use item processed at fewer points or under public monopoly. (Salt has been suggested as a nutrient carrier, but its use is often restricted during pregnancy and it can be extremely toxic to small children. Iodization of salt is, of course, highly effective and safe in controlling goiter in adults.)

Experimentation will show how far particular countries can move toward reducing their major nutritional deficiencies with such indirect or shotgun approaches as quantitative and qualitative improvements in food supply; public economic and

14. Dana G. Dalrymple, "Economic Aspects of Nutrition Improvement in Tunisia" (U.S. Department of Agriculture, 1970; processed).

educational action to raise private demand for protective foods or simply calories; marketing (with government support or encouragement) of new protective food formulations; and compulsory fortification of dietary staples. These approaches will help—faster in urban areas than rural, more in some countries than in others. But how much and how fast they will help those in greatest need is yet to be determined. There will inevitably be delays and some persistent shortfalls in reaching through these means the group that is also the hardest to reach through direct feeding programs: the infants and preschool children in impoverished rural households.

Direct Feeding Programs

Direct feeding of the most needy is the other major tool of nutrition policy. It is aimed directly at the vulnerable groups known to be suffering most from nutritional deficiencies. It carries nutrition education in its most practical and tangible form. Direct feeding raises few of the complex economic policy issues posed by attempts to intervene in agricultural or food production, marketing, and pricing to achieve nutritional objectives. In these senses, it seems to be the least speculative method.

But does it, in fact, work with measurable effectiveness? School lunch projects, the most widely used form of direct feeding, benefit 35 million children under aid programs sponsored by the United States. This is only a small fraction, however, of the hundreds of millions of such children in the developing countries. An unknown number of those who are served —some nutritionists say the vast majority—do not continually need dietary supplements or would not need them if their households made intelligent use of the foods available within their budgets. Extending school feeding programs to all children of this age group would entail a great administrative and financial effort. Discriminatory feeding of only the most needy within a student body raises difficult social and medical questions.

Costs of major school feeding programs are illustrated by Turkey's extensive efforts in cooperation with CARE and the U.S. government. This program in 1969 provided prepared meals, combining foods imported under U.S. Public Law 480 and local foods, to 2,240,000 school children each school day (180 days) for a total cost of nearly $21 million, or over $9 per recipient. U.S. food grants covered $8.8 million of these costs, local communities $11 million, and the central and local governments of Turkey about $1 million.

Clearly the first priority for such relatively expensive feeding efforts should go to the more vulnerable group, the infants, preschool children, and acutely malnourished mothers. This is the most difficult group to reach through fortification or market approaches. The delivery methods that have been attempted include outpatient and inpatient feeding in maternal and child health and nutritional rehabilitation centers, daily distribution through maternal and child health clinics, and less frequent distribution through health and welfare offices and women's associations.

The Title II/Voluntary Agency programs under Public Law 480 list about 8 million assumed recipients of maternal and preschool feeding services, at a cost of about $25 million annually in U.S. food ingredients alone. This is no more than a token effort, but it requires a vast outlay of scarce manpower skills in millions of individual delivery actions over a year's time.

The provision (as in parts of the Colombia program) of nutritious food along with health care and guidance on feeding and preventive medicine to mothers, infants, and preschool children is an attractive concept. Despite its cost and the possible diversion of scarce medical manpower to food-manage-

ment duties, a composite health–nutrition–population program may be the best way to deal with three unsolved
problems at once.

Teaming Nutrition Research and Action

Nutrition programs should be consciously treated as experiments in social change. If properly planned, staffed, and evaluated, these experiments should build the knowledge on which
larger, more complete attacks on hunger and nutritional diseases can be based. This has not often been their history. Baseline research and performance testing have been lacking in the
design of the traditional child-feeding and nutrition education
projects such as the UN-promoted applied nutrition projects.

Just as operational projects have lacked a research dimension
and output, so has nutrition research typically lacked a sharp
focus on the operational needs of the developers or managers
of nutrition programs. Individual pieces of research have, however, built a substantial body of knowledge that has both inspired and made more feasible the new movement toward
comprehensive nutrition strategies in developing countries.
With the advantage of hindsight, it is evident that nutrition
problems require a far more urgent and more efficient mobilization of social and natural scientists and closer teamwork between research, development policy, and nutrition programs
than anyone foresaw at the beginning of the last decade.

Economic development research in the past decade has almost ignored human nutrition, yet few questions could be
more relevant to development than the effects of proper nour-
ishment on the learning capacity, creativity, and productivity
of human beings. Health research has not been explicit in determining the economic costs of malnutrition to national
health budgets, much less to national production. Medical and

food science research has rarely dealt with the actual diets of
poor households of different sizes, income levels, and work
performance. Food technology research, quite productive in
devising new formulations, has been weak in developing the
practical means of getting new products into the dietary habits
of the poor. Nutrition surveys have stopped short of revealing
the actual nutrient composition of the diets of defined population groups. Consequently, agricultural research has not been
able to focus on exact nutrient deficiencies to be overcome by
plant breeding and adjustments in farm production.

These weaknesses suggest two of the prime functions of a
serious national nutrition policy: to challenge researchers and
their institutions to serve development strategy and program
operations, and to create a system for teaming the diverse social and technical specialists in comprehensive investigations
closely linked to experimental nutrition programs.

National and regional nutrition research and training institutes can meet part of this dual requirement. These institutes
cannot, however, be expected to staff or control all fields of research bearing on nutrition program choices. Exclusive reliance on a single institute, no matter how large and well staffed,
risks failure to mobilize the research capacity of universities,
medical schools, industry, and social science elements of many
government agencies. Reponsibility for mobilizing this wider
community of researchers and defining the main research
needs of a national nutrition policy is ideally lodged in the individual or group responsible for designing and monitoring the
experimental operations. In most countries this will be the
directorate of the national nutrition campaign, or a strong
chairman of a full-time interministerial committee on nutrition, or a development planning agency official, assisted in any
case by the national research council and the specialized nutrition research institute.

The research agenda will not be static, and it will differ in priorities from country to country. There are, however, some common themes that make it possible to lighten national research burdens through cooperative international action and coordination of national research programs. Much of the need for research in nutrition programs will be satisfied if the more conventional development research fields give proper attention to nutritional factors and if experts in these fields are engaged in designing and evaluating experimental nutrition programs.

Health Research

Highest priority in medical research should be assigned to exploring the interactions of malnutrition and infectious diseases and finding better means of breaking this vicious circle. A national development strategy needs reliable answers to these questions: How does malnutrition affect mental and physical development and individual learning and productive capacity? What effects do protein food supplements have on diets substantially short on calories?

Operational research on the most difficult delivery problem —reaching the poor mothers and small children whose staggering mortality and morbidity epitomize underdevelopment— should rank high on every nation's research agenda. It is a relatively small but logical step to integrate these health studies with a determination of the costs (including the diversion of scarce talent) and effectiveness of incorporating nutritional education, diet supplement services, and rehabilitation for malnutrition victims in comprehensive community health programs. Pilot projects testing separation of feeding and nutrition education from the general community health or maternal and child health delivery services should be as important to the health ministry as to the nutrition policy team as a whole.

Nutrition Surveys

The design of a general health program is equally as dependent as that of a multisectoral nutrition program on knowledge of the current state and causes of undernourishment and malnutrition. In either case the planner needs reliable baseline ("before") data against which he can evaluate effectiveness ("after"). This has become obvious to planners of food supplementation or feeding programs. It should be equally obvious to designers of mass public education campaigns to improve dietary habits, of schemes for subsidized marketing of enriched food formulations, of compulsory fortification, or of agricultural policy changes intended to reduce nutritional problems. To get these baseline facts, each country must undertake nutrition surveys of greater precision and reliability. Surveys also must establish physical growth norms. They should go beyond the standard assumptions about food values and test actual nutrient utilization and performance of representative samples of people living on different food combinations. Some countries should investigate what has actually caused the trend toward early weaning of infants and its consequences.

Nutrition surveys linked to operations need not always wait for extended pilot runs of a new project before testing results. In the case of the long-established school feeding programs, surveys can proceed immediately to draw on school records of physical and learning norms, where these exist, to get approximate answers to whether children served by these programs are bigger, stronger, and healthier as a result. More sophisticated study probably will be necessary, however, to answer such critical questions as whether mothers negate the school-feeding effort by giving less food at home to those served at school, or whether school feeding can be measurably differentiated from other environmental or family background factors making children better learners.

Agricultural Research

The nutrition research agenda also must assure that there is a serious shift to the qualitative aspects of agricultural production research. Little prodding is needed in most countries to direct agricultural research and experimental projects to the traditional problems of food supply—production, storage, processing, and preservation—or to the economic and social issues raised by the new technology. Nutrition policy should, however, explicitly assure more urgent attention to the economics and technology of crop diversification, breeding of higher protein quality into cereals, and practices promising higher productivity of protein-rich pulses and oilseeds.

In some countries, agricultural research can yield high returns by adapting the new glandless cottonseed to the local environment of soil and water limitations, pests, and diseases. Research to reduce the problems of toxic fungus growth on peanuts and the taste and flatulence problems with present varieties of legumes will be important in some countries. If oilseed protein is to be shifted substantially from animal to human consumption, there must be research on alternative fodder crops and the production of animal feeds based on single-cell proteins from such sources as petroleum-based hydrocarbons, molasses, or other industrial byproducts. Sesame seeds, which are high in sulfur-containing amino acids, could be a significant source of protein if agricultural research could develop a variety that yields more seed in a pod that does not burst before harvesting.

Food Technology Research

Food technology research extended the horizons for nutrition programs in the 1960s and entered the new decade with many promising opportunities under investigation. Its basic role is to produce for both market and direct feeding programs

a greater variety of lower cost enrichment ingredients, formulations, and processes exploiting local production advantages
and food preferences. Its priorities reflect the missions of sponsoring institutions and, in the case of private food industry research, the economic interests of particular companies. The
resulting diversity is highly desirable and should not be sacri-
ficed in the interests of a completely programmed national research effort.

One useful role for a national nutrition research program is
to engage the experience and judgment of private food entrepreneurs in defining nutritional goals and research priorities
for the whole community of social and technological specialists
who must be involved. Such collaboration should make food
technology research more relevant to operational needs and
facilitate government–industry cooperation in testing and
marketing of new products.

One of the main challenges to food technology research is
to develop a more nearly complete solution to the nutritional
deficiencies of the most vulnerable population groups through
fortification of staples. This demands reducing costs of synthetic methionine, tryptophan, threonine, and even lysine; reducing the cost and remaining undesirable characteristics of
vegetable and fish protein concentrates; and simplifying the
processes of fortification so as to make this technology available to small-scale, village-type mills or plants at low cost and
low risk of quality-control failures. In order to satisfy the preferences of the low-income market and the budget limitations
on that market and on government feeding programs, diversified choices and reduced costs should be sought for weaning
foods, enriched cereal formulations for older children and
adults, and other protective foods. Simple and inexpensive
means should be devised for processing and preserving natural
foods such as fish and beans in order to extend their geographical, seasonal, and income markets. The potential of leaf proteins and single-cell proteins grown on mineral hydrocarbons

for low-cost enrichment of human and animal diets should be determined and exploited. Animal and clinical testing for effectiveness and safety should be undertaken for all food formulations for the benefit of the world community.

Food technologists obviously must be a part of multidisciplinary teams assigned to operational research projects and evaluation of continuing programs. They should be teamed with agricultural researchers on such interlocking production-processing problems as the genetic improvement of cotton-seed, soybean, and sesame seed to reduce toxicity and flatulence problems. They also can help in anticipating and responding to technology-influenced changes in demand for farm products.

Opportunities for International Cooperation

Much of what has been done about malnutrition in the less developed countries and much of their present technical capacity to undertake comprehensive nutrition campaigns are attributable to international cooperation in scientific research, food technology, and feeding programs. The next stage in the elaboration of nutritional policies and programs will be a far more complex undertaking than the fragmentary and palliative efforts of the 1960s. It will demand more knowledge, more difficult judgments, more money, more trained people, and a rare degree of cooperation among separate bureaucracies and between government and industry.

As in other aspects of national development, most of the burden of research, planning, and action will fall on governmental organizations in the less developed countries. How can the international development-assistance agencies and professional organizations lighten that burden and minimize duplication of effort or error?

International agencies must learn to treat nutrition seriously as a development function and measure of success in their own doctrines and behavior. They must build their competence—not just that of a specialist group but of all professional and technical cadres—to understand nutrition's role in all aspects of development so as to participate intelligently in the developing countries' efforts to fight malnutrition. The administrative steps should include in-service training of agency staff, systematic circulation of literature on scientific, economic, and social aspects of nutrition in national development, seminars with nutrition program managers of developing countries, and inclusion of nutrition specialists in external consultant and contract teams dealing with health, agriculture, and other fields involved in nutritional improvement.

They should encourage creation of nutrition strategy bodies at points of power in the governments of developing countries. Without strong leadership and broadview concern with all aspects of the problem, a developing country is unlikely to discover the full range of foreign technical and financial assistance to nutritional development. Multilateral and bilateral aid agencies, by asking the right questions of governments in the developing countries, can stimulate the establishment of a central nutrition strategy organization, draw the attention of political and development leaders to nutrition problems and opportunities, and generally raise nutrition on the development policy agenda. The United Nations could support this process by holding an annual policy-level discussion of nutrition problems and programs in addition to the useful technical work of its Protein Advisory Group. The U.S. technical assistance agency should focus particularly on the provision of nutrition programming advisers and staff members to development planning organizations and relevant ministries in the developing countries.

Financial and technical aid should be provided for the establishment and operation of nutrition research and training institutes and programs in developing countries or in regional centers serving groups of smaller countries. Research and training will be most practical if it is closely connected with local operational and policy needs; this argues for national institutes rather than international wherever they can be supported and professionally staffed. However, the training and research services of the Institute of Nutrition of Central America and Panama have proved that regional institutes can offer practical services. Training also should be a deliberate objective of foreign research teams provided by aid agencies to national or regional institutes.

Conventional feeding, nutrition education, and applied nutrition assistance projects should be redesigned as operational experiments that produce reliable measurements of their effects on nutritional deficiencies and performance. The U.S. and UN programs should collaborate in periodic comparative reviews of the research methodology and findings of these experiments.

Nutrition policy should be made one dimension of advisory, research, and operational projects in health, agriculture, and urban or rural development fields financed through technical assistance. Obviously, the positive endorsement of the host agencies concerned is a necessity. Nutrition is more likely to be accepted and have some effect where a dynamic nutrition policy or strategy body is influencing ministerial programs.

Aid agencies should plan and support programs of international comparative research in several crucial areas of food science and human nutrition. Those questions having the greatest bearing on the future directions of nutrition policy probably are: Does the addition of protein or amino acids to otherwise unchanged diets of adults and older children in low-income Asian, African, and Latin American communities significantly improve their health and performance? Does fortification of staple foods bring about a significant reduction in protein–calorie malnutrition among the infants, preschool children, and mothers in low-income urban and rural families whose total food budgets remain unchanged? What are the extent, severity, and long-term consequences of mental and psychomotor retardation caused by protein deficiencies in infants and preschool children?

The international programs should be guided by a single professional manager or committee designated by the financing agency, but they should engage experts of the developing countries and local research and operating agencies in both their design and execution. In addition, the aid agencies should assure that international collaborative research schemes in agriculture and health provide usable knowledge and processes for nutrition programs in the developing countries.

Aid agencies should be willing to use their funds to support research by private food industries as well as public agencies, in developing countries as well as at home, on the technological processes of food fortification, production of fortifying agents, food preservation, and formulation. If publicly financed, the products of this research should be made freely available without licensing fee.

Summary

Protein–calorie malnutrition and other dietary deficiencies are root causes, as well as symptoms, of the plight of many less developed countries. Their efforts to achieve better health, education, or productivity will be incomplete until nutrition gains a secure place in national development strategies and is represented by strong leadership.

Comprehensive nutrition programs began to take shape in several pioneering countries during the late 1960s. Their examples and the growing availability of nutritional knowledge and technological tools should stimulate other countries to initiate systematic programs in the 1970s. Substantial budgetary outlays and economic tradeoffs are clearly warranted for major research and experimental efforts in nutrition. In some countries there are urgent and economically attractive opportunities for operational and policy measures that go beyond experimentation.

A national nutritional strategy normally will include efforts to improve basic food production, both quantitatively and qualitatively; public economic and educational measures to raise demand for food, particularly protective foods, among lower income groups; public action to encourage or support marketing of new protective food formulations; compulsory fortification of dietary staples; and direct feeding of vulnerable groups, preferably coupled with nutritional education and sometimes with other health services. The results of controlled experiments, supported by additional research, should point the way to the most effective and financially acceptable combination of full-scale programs in each country.

This survey has suggested six steps for U.S. and multilateral technical assistance: equipping the assistance agencies themselves with specialized competence and broad comprehension of nutritional aspects of development; encouraging and aiding the creation of nutrition strategy bodies at points where development policy and budgets are made in the developing countries; supporting the establishment of nutrition research and training institutes or programs in the developing countries and regions; adapting the conventional feeding and nutrition-education projects to produce information on the relative effectiveness of various approaches to the most pressing needs; incorporating nutritional objectives in agricultural, health, urban, and rural development projects; and carrying out major international programs of comparative research on some of the central issues in food science and human nutrition.

The emergence of nutrition as a recognized test and target of national development will open new opportunities for constructive international service by American scientists, educators, and health and welfare specialists, and a broad range of U.S. institutions. This nascent movement offers the United States an attractive means of mobilizing private and public action on a problem central to both the economic and humanitarian goals of development.

CHAPTER SEVEN

New Directions
in Educational Development

EDUCATION was in many respects development's biggest business and the source of its most widely sensed disappointments in the 1960s. Much was done, but when the decade was over the gap between hopes and realities was wide. It was obvious by the 1970s that more of the same would not do; more efficient and relevant education and new approaches to educational financing were required. It was less obvious how the developing countries and international assistance agencies could better work together in translating new ideas into low-cost operations.

The 1960s began with enthusiastic confidence in education —almost any kind—as a reforming force for social justice and economic modernization. The less developed countries, trying to overcome centuries of neglect of their human resources, sought salvation in crash efforts to duplicate the educational systems of the richer countries. Schooling was expected to provide literacy, to unshackle minds for change, to produce cadres of leaders, managers, technicians, and skilled workers for modern life. If expatriate technicians, teachers, or bureaucrats of a former metropole must be replaced, then establish universities and technical schools. If farming practices must change, teach agriculture in the schools and set up an agricultural extension service. If health must be improved, teach hygiene and nutrition to mothers and children in schools, in community centers, by radio or poster. If the birth rate must be lowered, teach parents birth control.

The decade closed with that faith in quick educational answers to complex development problems widely discredited. Perhaps this was inevitable and good; one of the universal truths of education is that government and public alike expect too much of it. They want schools to equip new generations to meet changing individual and social challenges, to overcome all sorts of environmental handicaps, but at the same time to preserve traditional ways and values—all this at bargain prices. Generally, governments are more interested in demonstrable quantitative progress than in the quality or effectiveness of new public institutions.

Quantitative progress there was, and it should not be discounted. But as schools multiplied and their staffs and budgets mounted, it became apparent that with present methods and available resources the goals could not be reached. Neither the egalitarian ideal of education for all nor immediate manpower-training needs of development in agriculture, health, industry, or other sectors were being met despite impressive effort.

Growth Pains

In nearly every developing country the educational growth chart turned steeply upward during the 1960s. In Latin America alone, more than 250,000 primary school classrooms were built and more than 1.3 million teachers were added in primary and secondary schools.[1] The number of students enrolled in formal schooling in the noncommunist developing countries rose by about 6–7 percent annually.[2] Yet, by the end of the

1. Agency for International Development (AID), *Summary Economic and Social Indicators, 18 Latin American Countries, 1960–69* (June 1970).

2. Adapted from International Institute for Educational Planning

decade nearly 300 million children between the ages of five
and fourteen were not in school—considerably more than were
enrolled (see Table 7-1).[3] Explosive population growth reflected in high (typically nearly one-to-one) ratios of depen-
dent-aged children to producers, coupled with an initial lack of
any schooling for the majority, forced these countries to race
in order to gain slowly on their educational goals.

Secondary school enrollment grew twice as fast as primary,
but from such small beginnings that by 1970 less than 10 percent of Africans in the fifteen to nineteen age group (only a
fraction of 1 percent in the least developed countries) and a
little over one-fourth of this group in other developing regions
were attending secondary schools.[4] Even so, in many countries,
new job opportunities were not acceptable to the holders of
secondary and higher education diplomas who thought they
had earned tickets to elite careers. From the problem of acute
shortages of educated manpower, some countries lurched into
a new problem of what to do with their "educated unem-
ployed." (Of course, this is a structural problem of much
broader ramifications than the educational system.)

The search for ways to make education directly serve development led many countries to vocational schooling—upper
primary and secondary level alternatives to general education.
These schools added to the enrollment figures but it is questionable whether many of them added much to development.
The better ones managed to impart some useful general education along with skills. To a discouraging (but not absolute)

(IIEP), "Memorandum Concerning Research to be Undertaken on the
Financing of Educational Costs in Developing Countries" (Paris: United
Nations Educational, Scientific and Cultural Organization [UNESCO],
October 1970; processed).

   3. Adapted from 1970 projections in *UNESCO Statistical Yearbook,
1968* (Paris: UNESCO, 1969).
   4. AID, "Comparisons between Developed and Less Developed Areas"
(1970; processed).

TABLE 7-1. *School Enrollment Ratios in Selected Countries, 1967*

| | Percent of age group enrolled | |
Region and country	Primary school	Secondary school
Africa		
Algeria	68	8
Cameroon[a]	82	6
Chad[a]	31	2
Congo (Kinshasa)[a]	90	6
Ethiopia	13	3
Ghana	90	14
Guinea[b]	31	5
Ivory Coast	66	8
Kenya	60	7
Liberia	69	9
Mali	26	5
Morocco	55	12
Nigeria[a]	36	3
Tunisia	106[c]	19
Uganda[a]	46	11
United Arab Republic	71	30
Tanzania	38	2
Central America		
Costa Rica[a]	110[c]	31
Dominican Republic	97	18
El Salvador	93	13
Guatemala	58	10
Honduras[a]	83	8
Mexico	98	18
Nicaragua[a]	73	15
Panama	104[c]	38
South America		
Argentina	101[c]	39
Bolivia	87	21
Brazil	123[c]	20
Chile	103[c]	25
Colombia	90	20
Ecuador	94	20
Peru	109[c]	36

TABLE 7-1.—*Continued*

| Region and country | Percent of age group enrolled | |
	Primary school	Secondary school
Asia		
Afghanistan	19	3
Cambodia	84	10
China (Taiwan)	104[c]	42
India[b]	56	13
Indonesia	72	11
Iran	58	19
Korea, Republic of	104[c]	34
Laos	45	2
Pakistan[a]	41	18
Philippines[b]	109[c]	39
Thailand	80	13
Turkey	75	26
Viet-Nam, Republic of	92	25

Source: United Nations, Educational, Scientific and Cultural Organization, *UNESCO Statistical Yearbook*, 1969 (Paris: UNESCO, 1970).
  a. Ratios are based on 1966 enrollment.
  b. Ratios are based on 1965 enrollment.
  c. Percentages are inflated by repeaters or others outside the officially defined school ages for primary or secondary schools.

extent, the formal vocational schools produced graduates poorly trained for fields in which jobs did not exist on the scale the planners had expected or for such fields as farming in which the youngster either never was interested or lost interest during training. Their staffs and equipment, while typically poor, nevertheless cost three to five times as much per student as general secondary education.

The greatest costs, however, were reflected in dropout and repeater rates in primary and, to a lesser extent, secondary schooling. Only a minority of those enrolled in primary school advanced far enough to establish basic "three Rs" education for life. In India and Pakistan, to take two large examples, fewer than one-third as many pupils were enrolled in the fifth grade, the last year of primary school, as in the first grade in 1966.[5] The majority of school beginners had dropped out before they had a chance to establish literacy. In equatorial and tropical Africa, less than one-fourth of the children who were six years old in 1960 completed the fourth grade, the minimum for achievement of literacy.[6]

The dropout and repeater rates reflected negative parental attitudes or examples, unstimulating instruction or misguided examination systems; often, however, the main cause was the simple lack of an accessible school. In the villages of developing countries there is no school of any sort for children beyond grade two in a shocking number of instances, grade three or four in most. It is a rare country that offers a complete primary schooling to rural children within reach of their homes. In some relatively prosperous Latin American countries whose political doctrines eloquently express egalitarian concepts, the poor farm child who cannot afford boarding school or has no willing relatives in town has no chance of going beyond the third or fourth grade. Where there is a complete primary school, this is the terminal opportunity for most children beyond walking reach of a town. Even where secondary schooling is accessible, most rural children are screened out by academic entrance requirements, fees, or sheer shortage of space. City children have better opportunity, but the same screening process handicaps the poor, the less motivated, or those whose parents do not value education.

Attempts to overcome shortages in all levels of public education cost the developing countries major portions—in some cases two-thirds—of their national fiscal growth during at least the first half of the 1960s (see Table 7-2). Their public outlays on education grew, on the average, at about twice the rate of their growth in national income in the 1950s but slowed in the

5. AID, NESA *Educational Profiles* (May 1969).
6. IIEP, "Memorandum Concerning Research."

TABLE 7-2. *Public Expenditures on Education, 1967*[a]

Country and region	As percent of GNP	As percent of total expenditures
Africa		
Algeria[b]	4.9	18.7
Cameroon[c]	2.9	11.3
Chad	3.6	14.3
Congo (Kinshasa)	n.a.	20.8
Ethiopia	1.4	n.a.
Ghana[d]	4.6	n.a.
Guinea[c, d]	n.a.	19.4
Ivory Coast[d]	5.0	20.4
Kenya[d]	5.6	18.4
Liberia[b]	n.a.	13.8
Mali	3.6	19.5
Morocco[b]	3.6	16.2
Nigeria[d]	2.5	n.a.
Tunisia[e]	5.0	24.5
Uganda	2.9	12.5
United Arab Republic[e]	5.3	19.1
Central America		
Costa Rica	4.1	n.a.
Dominican Republic[f]	2.3	n.a.
El Salvador[c]	2.7	25.4
Guatemala	2.0	17.4
Honduras[d]	2.9	n.a.
Mexico	2.5	n.a.
Nicaragua	2.7	18.1
Panama[b]	3.4	23.2
South America		
Bolivia	3.5	28.9
Brazil[b, e]	1.0	7.5
Chile[e]	3.9	9.0
Colombia[e]	2.3	13.6
Ecuador	2.8	21.5
Peru	3.4	n.a.
Asia		
Cambodia	n.a.	21.6
Ceylon[e]	4.4	n.a.
China (Taiwan)	3.1	19.3
India[d]	2.6	n.a.

TABLE 7-2.—*Continued*

Country and region	As percent of GNP	As percent of total expenditures
Indonesia	n.a.	n.a.
Iran	2.4	6.2
Korea, Republic of	2.4	18.1
Laos	n.a.	10.2
Pakistan[e]	1.2	6.8
Philippines[b]	2.8	n.a.
Thailand[c, e]	2.8	14.9
Turkey[b]	3.5	20.0
Viet-Nam, Republic of	1.2	5.4

Source: *UNESCO Statistical Yearbook, 1969.*
n.a.: Not available.
a. Includes public expenditures on public and, where applicable, on subsidized private education for all countries.
b. Includes Ministry of Education expenditures only.
c. Includes central (or federal) government expenditures only.
d. Expenditures for 1965.
e. Expenditures for 1966.
f. Expenditures for 1963.

1960s as competition for budget funds intensified. Educational budgets had to rise at spectacular rates in countries with the most acute financial limitations because they tended to be furthest behind in the literacy and schooling race. Their unit costs of education were heightened by the premium salaries qualified teachers could command, ranging from three to twenty times their countries' per capita incomes, compared with about twice per capita incomes in the more broadly educated societies. Ambitious goals of more and better education for all were plainly unattainable in the time frames these countries had originally established.

Public expenditures on education in Africa climbed from 3 percent to 4.3 percent of these countries' gross national products (GNP), and from 14.5 percent to 16.4 percent of their national budgets, on the average, between 1960 and 1965. In Asia, the 1965 figures were just under 3 percent of GNP and

14 percent of total budgets.[7] In Latin America, where much education is privately or church financed, central government outlays on education amounted to just over 2 percent of GNP in 1969 as well as in 1965, and some 13 percent of national budgets, on the average, in both 1965 and 1969. (These figures are depressed by the exclusion of state government contributions in Brazil. They also conceal wide disparities; for example, Brazil put only 6 percent of its central government budget into education, Uruguay 30 percent.)[8] Even without taking into account educational expenditures outside central government budgets, Latin American governments spent two-and-one-half times as much on education as on agriculture in the late 1960s.

Despite this impressive financial commitment, interim targets in primary and secondary enrollment set for the two-decade period, 1960–80,[9] had not been reached. By 1970, countries of all three regions that had established goals in conferences sponsored by the UN Educational, Scientific and Cultural Organization (UNESCO) had fallen so far behind schedule that it was obvious the goals retained little weight in determining national educational plans and budgets. These countries evidently were unwilling to double or treble their education budgets in the 1970s, the price most of them would have to pay to achieve the goal of primary school enrollment opportunity for all and enrollment of 25–35 percent (depending on the region) of the age group in secondary schools. For some countries, money was not the only bottleneck: to replace unqualified primary teachers with secondary school graduates would require more teachers than the entire output of their secondary schools.

7. Ibid., as amended by *UNESCO Statistical Yearbook, 1969,* Table 2.18.

8. AID, *Summary Economic and Social Indicators.*

9. Organization for Economic Cooperation and Development (OECD), Development Assistance Committee, "Educational Assistance Needs" (Paris: OECD, March 1968; processed).

Beyond the Numbers

By the end of the decade, critiques of the quality and purposes of the school systems were indicating the need for fundamental reforms. The executive secretary of the UN Economic Commission for Africa felt that rural education had "failed dismally" to spark "an ability and willingness of the rural people to transform their physical and social environments."[10] Another observer, stressing the "futility" of conventional schooling in Latin America as a force for equalizing opportunity, proposed a radically different system of education. He would sandwich or mix education with work, and extend it well beyond conventional school ages, to force it to become more responsive to its consumers' needs.[11]

African leaders, while justifiably proud of their enormous progress in establishing universities and teacher-training institutions and replacing expatriates in both teaching and administrative positions, began to criticize the content of their education, calling for reappraisals of primary and teacher training curricula. Political leaders, attacking the inherited European system, lamented the continued emphasis on preparation for the next level of formal education, which few children could hope to enter. Teaching methods and curricula were accommodated to academic entrance exams copied from European systems, militating against syllabuses oriented to the local environment and to agricultural and mechanical work.

Uncertainty and wishful thinking in dealing with such problems led to decisions to set up separate vocational or agricultural schools or to substitute superficial study of farming and

10. Robert K. Gardiner, address at Commonwealth Conference on Education in Rural Areas, University of Ghana (Legon, 1970).

11. Ivan Illich, "The Futility of Schooling in Latin America," *Saturday Review*, April 20, 1968.

crafts for general educational content in the upper primary and secondary grades. As a result, farm youth and slow-learning city youth were prematurely shunted into schooling that denied them a solid educational foundation in favor of a smattering of skills. Some countries stuck with general education, enlivening their curricula with illustrations drawn from local experience; their better schools taught both town and country children the place of agriculture, commerce, and industry in the nation's life.

Efforts to improve teaching led to crash training and retraining programs. All agreed that too little effort had gone into adapting and localizing secondary education to serve development needs, especially teacher training at the secondary level. Foreign assistance began to concentrate on breaking this bottleneck in the supply of teachers and other skilled manpower, especially for rural services. Special effort was devoted to revising textbooks and chipping away at the shortage of every sort of teaching material. Some pursued the hope that modern educational technology might permit a great qualitative leap forward at low cost.

In many quarters by the end of the 1960s, a widespread sense of deepening crisis made radical remedies almost a necessity, as the following analysis implies:

Rising social demand is out of balance with educational capacity; educational output is getting increasingly out of balance with manpower requirements and the supply of jobs; the curriculum and teaching methods are woefully ill-fitted to the real needs of students and to their wide individual differences; educational administration is obsolete and overwhelmed by its new and large tasks; educational resource needs are growing rapidly beyond resource availabilities.

To escape from this educational crisis, nations must first of all abandon their simplistic strategy of "linear expansion" which mainly calls for making the existing educational system rapidly larger in its traditional image; they must instead adopt a strategy of educational change and innovation, calculated to make more efficient use of educational resources, and to adapt educational structures, content and methods to the dynamically changing needs and circumstances of the world around them.[12]

Strategic Options

The demand for new development strategies and fundamental change, heard in every sector, is particularly compelling in education. The budgetary crunch is forcing a rethinking of the automatic priority that education has held for two decades. Public policy makers and critics outside the education establishments are pressing for better educational means of closing the productivity gaps between the rich and poor nations. Serious efforts to chart new directions in education thus seem likely in the 1970s.

The basic strategic choices are intensely political: What kind of society is to be built? Is education to be regarded as a basic human right, the foundation of a meritocracy? How much should government intervene to equalize social and economic opportunity through schooling of the young and continuing education of all age groups? Should the educational system be biased toward the primarily economic objective of manpower training for occupational slots in a system designed by government? Should there be one kind of education for rural living, intended to discourage flight to the cities, and another for urban living, or rather a common basic education for social and economic mobility? Should the central government accept the risks of decentralized or community control of educational content or administration?

12. P. H. Coombs, "Research for Educational Planning," in William J. Platt (ed.), *Research for Educational Planning: Notes on Emergent Needs* (Paris: UNESCO, 1970), App. D, and *The World Educational Crisis: A Systems Analysis* (Oxford University Press, 1968).

The allocative questions that follow must be resolved within narrow budgetary margins, with a mixture of political and economic judgments. Proposals for increased educational spending must compete with claims on the budget from agriculture, industry, health, population and nutrition programs, or transportation, electric power, or other services. Within education, choices must be made between quantity and quality, formal and nonformal, general and technical, primary, secondary, and higher education, total financing and shared-cost financing, and so on.

In practical fact the political bedrock or basic strategy of education is never drastically altered by budgetary reviews and only rarely by longer term policy-planning exercises. Nevertheless, change does occur in the process of revising or restating educational policy or in launching new attacks on old problems. That is the main prospect for the 1970s.

In their search for more rational goals and methods, developing countries will be influenced by the experience of other countries and the opportunities afforded by foreign assistance to make fresh starts. The role of foreign assistance is not to make national education strategies but to make it easier for national governments to undertake promising improvements in their strategies. Collaboration will obviously be more fruitful in developing countries committed to a course of pragmatic effort to find better paths to economic and social progress. In these countries the political climate will be favorable not only for international collaboration, but for objective research and evaluation and for experimentation with educational methods that break with tradition.

Bracketing the Targets

The concern of development assistance is not education, per se, but the strategies and methods of human resource development that governments of developing nations can use to achieve major economic and social objectives. This excludes education as an avocation or ornament of the elite, or education as an object of international cultural or political exchange. It includes both formal schooling and such deliberate, organized nonformal education as agricultural extension, adult literacy training, and in-service staff training by industrial employers, labor unions, and government. The occasional, unorganized flows of information and ideas through publications, radio, television, motion pictures, and personal communication, although important means of education, are not primary subjects of technical assistance. Also excluded from consideration here are the requirements for a sharpened educational attack on critical professional and technical manpower shortages in agricultural, health, population, and nutrition programs; these are best considered in programs focused on each of those sectors.

This restrictive definition of educational development leaves plenty of problems. Most developing countries must decide how best to determine the share of public budgets that should be devoted to education relative to other sectors, and to each major subsector of human resource development, taking into account social and political demands as well as development benefits. They must also decide how to make education more efficient, both productively and administratively, and how to measure efficiency against an evolving society's needs. They must learn to mobilize and tap financial resources for education outside the central government's education budget, and to exploit new educational technologies to compensate for shortages of good teachers, poor environmental stimuli for learning, or limited extramural learning opportunities, without substantially raising the cost of educational output.

They must learn how to reconcile society's need for practical, work-oriented education with the concept of equal educational opportunity and social mobility; or, how to relate a student's education to his background, community environment, and likely future employment without prematurely consigning him to a niche. They must determine how to make use of actual industrial, agricultural, and service employment experience and facilities to provide skill and literacy training to adults and school dropouts, and more generally, how to use the whole array of public service programs, on-the-job training, and other nonformal educational tools to develop human resources outside the formal school system.

Ten years ago broad philosophical questions and narrow pedagogical issues figured prominently in technical assistance. Most countries today have a small corps of educational philosophers and administrators who have attended graduate schools abroad, read the literature, participated in international conferences, and reached their own conclusions. Many of them understand better than foreigners the local political constraints, educational doctrines, and resource shortages that perpetuate the irrationalities in their systems. They also have learned that general advice from a foreign educational expert usually leaves them with the problems nicely redefined but unsolved.

These countries now need—in some cases, want—financial and technical help in carrying out programs to correct or bypass specific problems. (For example, in devising and trying a new way of consolidating the literacy of grade school dropouts.) They need, but often cannot undertake because of budgetary or staff limitations, experimental projects to test particular applications of various educational technologies.

Governments as a whole sometimes need the catalyzing force of a thorough self-study (not another foreign educationist study) of their educational problems, required in the application for foreign assistance, or a pilot project supported by a foreign agency, to cut through inhibitions or jurisdictional hangups.

All the developing countries need a practical, rapid system of international cooperative research to help them select promising answers to specific educational questions. The developing countries' specialists and institutions as well as experts of the aid-giving countries should be actively engaged in intercountry comparative research, and their findings should be rapidly circulated.

Some countries need and want professional staff from abroad—not advisers—to design and work on innovative projects or to fill temporary gaps in institutions of research, planning, and training. Technical assistance can also help to devise administratively feasible job-census techniques that will describe skills currently in demand and the use of training already offered. This information, obtained annually or biannually, would be far more reliable guides for both formal and nonformal education than prospective, long-range manpower estimates.

Another needed institutional innovation that foreign assistance might plant and propagate is a network linking teacher education with research and field advisory or extension services. Such a network could provide a two-way flow of information, ideas, and techniques among practitioners, analysts, and managers of education similar to that of the better agricultural research–extension–training systems. The absence of close linkages designed to promote continuing gains in efficiency in education may account for much of what ails many school systems.

Foreign assistance expended on routine and marginal increments of general support for educational systems as they are will not be fruitful. The main thrust of U.S. or multilateral assistance policy should be to seek out, encourage, and support promising local innovations. This is not to suggest attempts to bring about a wholesale dismemberment of educational systems, but rather to help systems adapt to current demand more rapidly and rationally.

A panel of experts convened by the International Institute for Educational Planning (IIEP) recommended to the multilateral aid agencies that priority go to projects in which:

the applicant proposes to depart from conventional practice and to blaze new trails, thus helping to test and apply new educational features available to all. Such a policy would give needed incentives to break away from traditional patterns that have proved inadequate and obsolete. It might release the creative instincts of present international educational experts and attract new ones who are convinced that educational change is imperative and are anxious to participate in giving it impetus. Perhaps more important, it would give the weight of international approval and support to the whole notion of educational change and innovation.[13]

One of the IIEP panelists proposed an ambitious agenda for change (which may be appropriate for the more advanced developing countries):

1. *The modernization of educational management*—including the recruitment and training of skilled management teams of appropriate specialists; the development and application of more adequate instruments for diagnosing, planning and evaluating the performance of educational systems and subsystems; and new procedures to ensure much wider participation in planning and decision-making by lower echelon administrators, teachers, students and interested members of the general public.

2. *The modernization of teachers*—including far-reaching reforms of teacher recruitment and training, changes in salary structures and in teacher functions, and the opening up of new career development opportunities for the ablest teachers.

3. *The modernization of content and the learning process*— including drastic reforms of the curriculum, abandoning the chronological grade system and self-contained classroom, innovations in the methods of teaching and learning—all with a view to achieving

13. Coombs, "Research for Educational Planning."

individualized education within the context of mass education so as to give real meaning to the idea of equal educational opportunity.

4. *Increased emphasis on "non-formal" education*—integrating it with formal education in order to make lifelong learning an efficient and rewarding process and, in the case of poorer countries, to provide opportunities for people deprived of formal education.[14]

Educational Research

The potential contributions of educational research have been poorly realized in developing nations. Strong educational research capability, particularly operational research, does not exist in any developing country or international center. A few U.S. and European research centers have given some attention to problems involved in the educational dilemmas of poorer countries, but their staff capacities are small and their links with counterparts or operations in the developing countries very limited. Most educational research has been descriptive and theoretical, more concerned with small bits of the system than with the whole.

The limited contributions of research to educational management are blamed on the complexity of the issues, each with a multitude of human variables difficult to control or measure; the inherently conservative climate of education and its lack of research–operational linkages; weak personal incentives for undertaking large-scale operational research or experimental programs in many countries; and the tight education budgets in less developed countries, which squeeze such "nonessential" functions as research and experimentation.

Such useful research findings and innovative experiments as are produced are disseminated by educational journals that sel-

14. Ibid.

dom reach the attention of those outside the establishment.[15] (UNESCO and the regional UN economic development commissions are missing an opportunity for useful service in not translating the best of current technical reports on educational research and innovative practices into short papers that will be read and understood by a wider audience in all the developing countries.)

The emergence of educational planning as a field of higher education and an aspect of government administration holds promise of stimulating more policy-oriented research and providing a link between research and operations. That alone will not necessarily induce research to become more inventive, however.

Better funding of educational research would help. Only small fractions of 1 percent of education budgets now are allocated to research. But without a system for assuring that research will be mounted and staffed on the scale required and focused on the key problems of educational planning and management, more money could yield only a larger volume of fragmentary data. Cooperative international research programs addressing key problems, such as those supported by UNESCO's regional centers and the IIEP or by general development agencies, can help in establishing discipline, but they are even more difficult than national programs to gear closely to operations and the decision-making process.

The ideal network of research, experimental development, training, and extension is much more easily described than instituted and competently staffed. It is probably a more realistic goal for the 1970s to try to build pieces of such national networks where motivations and capacity are strongest and to supplement the process by international action.

15. For a comprehensive treatment of this issue, see Ladislav Cerych, "Accelerating the Innovation Process in Education," in G. Z. F. Bereday (ed.), *Essays on World Education* (Oxford University Press, 1969), pp. 34–50.

International development assistance agencies ought to work to create demand for problem-solving research and planning by requiring thorough identification of problems and alternative solutions in proposals for broad educational sector assistance. If the climate for problem-oriented research is to be improved, it should be made a major part of the training of educational administrators and teachers in programs supported by foreign assistance. Research and planning for comprehensive rural and urban development programs, normally under the jurisdiction of agencies other than the education ministry, should include educational elements.

Expertise in educational innovation for developing countries should be built through long-term research and training grants to competent U.S. institutions. Individual experts (including iconoclasts) and institutions of the developing countries should be encouraged and given aid to participate in international comparative field research sponsored by the UNESCO regional centers, IIEP, or specialized educational research or advisory institutions of the donor countries. Through IIEP and the UNESCO centers, wider publicity should be given to educational innovations, current research that may help developing countries, and reappraisals of research priorities.

Technical assistance devoted to these measures, rather than traditional research units of teacher training institutions, is most likely to generate stronger "market demand" for fresh ideas and openings for innovators.

Assistance for innovative projects should as a subsidiary purpose deliberately stimulate the growth of a research–planning–training–extension network. For example, a new program of nonformal education should include experimental research functions and follow-up evaluation of results, feedback of findings to teacher training institutions, and application of any applicable findings on the learning process to other parts of the educational system. Teacher training institutions should be encouraged to detail staff and advanced students to do some of this evaluative work and incorporate findings in their own curricula. Local teacher education institutions should, in some situations, be the chosen instrument for carrying out the research component of education projects financed by U.S. aid.

These suggestions amount to indirect and piecemeal rather than frontal approaches to the strengthening of educational research in the developing countries. They are based on the assumption that research as a component of current operations will be more relevant to public policy than the findings of a separate institution are likely to be.

Innovative Programs

If experimental or innovative programs are adopted as the main thrust of international collaboration on educational development in the 1970s, they must be addressed to a country's truly critical problems, not just the generality of educational modernization. "Innovation" must not become either a slogan for dressing up old styles of technical assistance in new jargon or an excuse for financing transient fashions in educational theory. Nor should the requirement of a thorough analysis of the educational and development context be set aside in favor of piecemeal attacks on problems.

The preparatory study and design of projects should assure a reasonable prospect of producing workable improvements that can be multiplied widely within the country and possibly more broadly. Each project should include provision for continuing research and evaluation so that applicable lessons can be recorded quickly and applied in the next steps of the project and disseminated to other interested countries.

Assistance usually must include substantial financial as well as technical resources. Real financial limitations and tradition-bound budget or educational finance policies obstruct experimentation in most countries. If experimental projects are intended to serve the international community, and if the educational crisis is viewed as urgent, some of the operating costs of projects, as well as investment and technical expenses, must be borne by outsiders. Financial as well as technical agencies of donor governments and groups should participate in the planning of assistance to these projects.

Some recent pioneering efforts suggest the range of potential innovative programs and their special characteristics.

Performance-Incentive Budgeting

Brazil launched in 1970 a comprehensive educational modernization program with the help of a $50 million education sector loan from the U.S. Agency for International Development (AID) covering both capital and technical assistance. Its broad objectives were to improve the management and increase the efficiency of primary and secondary education; to provide educational services to large segments of the school-age population not then served; and to make primary and secondary education more relevant to prospective employment opportunities and manpower requirements. The principal new mechanism for stimulating and guiding modernization was a national Education Development Fund, which consolidated all federal programs of support for the Brazilian states' primary and secondary schools and established a system of annual awards to help finance the states' educational improvement plans.

Under the scheme, 10 percent of the fund was reserved for bonus awards to states demonstrating outstanding performance against such specific measurements as lowered cost per unit of learning achievement; reduction in the number of late starters, repeaters, and dropouts; successful experimentation with new instructional procedures; and improved utilization of instructional materials. At least 15 percent of each state plan was to be for acquisition of instructional materials. An additional 10 percent of the fund was reserved for support of experimental projects aimed at increasing the effectiveness of educational expenditures. These could include innovations in teacher training in new media or methods; urban school experiments with increased numbers of students per teacher, programmed learning, individualized paced instruction, and team teaching; and bus transportation for consolidating rural primary schools and new curricula for such schools.

The program covered advanced training in the United States or Brazil of educational administrators, and local contracting for the preparation of uniform achievement tests, revised syllabuses, and instructional methodguides.[16]

A sectoral reform program need not, and in most cases should not, be as complex as Brazil's, but it will by definition involve multiple innovations in a variety of settings. A thorough sectoral study, with or without the aid of foreign consultants, and an independent analysis prepared by the assisting agency should precede negotiation of the plan of cooperation and aid terms. Aid agencies should resist the temptation to believe that their money gives them infinite wisdom in judging a country's educational plans.

Refinement and Extension of Reforms

Ambitious educational innovations sometimes have withered or died when unexpected problems arose or when planned supporting or follow-up actions were frustrated by lack of competent staff or funds. Others have not been generally adopted

16. AID, "Brazil—Education Sector Loan II" (1970).

because of a lack of financing or skilled manpower that need not have been permanent. Foreign assistance interposed in such situations can yield high returns. The continuation of AID educational sector lending to Chile in the late 1960s illustrates this kind of program.

Chile began carrying out in the mid-1960s perhaps the most thoroughgoing educational reform any nation has attempted over a short period. The plan called for complete modernization of curriculum in the first eight years of basic education; curriculum changes in the four years of secondary level general and vocational programs, providing for a common core of general education and mobility between the two tracks; greatly increased use of teaching materials; expansion of in-service teacher training and counseling; and improvement of preservice teacher preparation. It aimed at immediate achievement of universal primary education through grade six; an increase in secondary school enrollment from 28 percent of the school-age population in 1965 to 35 percent by 1970 and 50 percent by 1975; nearly a doubling of total enrollment in higher education; and initiation of a repayment plan to recoup from university graduates a substantial part of their higher educational costs.

All of this required an array of new supporting institutions, notably a National Supervision Service with 130 field offices and a National Guidance Service, which together amount to an extension service; a National Evaluation Service and a National Center for Retraining of Teachers, Curriculum and Didactic Materials Development; a Higher Education Planning Council; a National Commission for Scientific and Technological Research; and new management and technical offices in the Education Ministry.

U.S. assistance was provided to permit accelerated action on all fronts. Additional technical assistance was focused on problems that developed in carrying out curriculum changes, in guidance, testing, and evaluation services, in preparation of secondary vocational teachers, and in development of instructional materials.[17]

Teacher Education

Innovations in the education of educators and in the roles of pedagogical institutions rank near the top of any list of educational modernization opportunities for international cooperation. "Irrelevant education results largely from teaching teachers to teach irrelevant things—to propagate unrealistic values and to cling to educational traditionalism. . . . It seems clear that to relate education more effectively to development needs there is a prime requirement for a reorientation of teacher-training."[18]

A model in this field is the Northern Nigeria Teacher-Education Project, supported initially by the Ford Foundation and later by AID, which has demonstrated ways of stretching the supply of qualified teachers. Experts from the University of Wisconsin, working with counterparts from seven Nigerian teacher training colleges, have tested large group and team teaching, inexpensive programmed materials, language laboratory teaching and other uses of audio-visual materials, and expanded use of teacher-interns. Elementary and secondary school personnel as well as university faculty members have conducted the supporting research and evaluation. The project evidently has brought lasting changes in the attitudes of key Nigerian educators toward educational innovation as well as diffusion of new materials and methods of teacher training.

International assistance can hasten the expansion, refinement, and wider use of programs to sensitize teachers to the requirements and processes of national development, enabling

17. AID, "Chile Education Sector Loan" (1968).
18. John F. Hilliard, unpublished staff paper, AID (1970).

them to stress opportunities for students to work in development activities. Such programs are in operation or being established in Ethiopia, Kenya, Uganda, and Tanzania.

Ethiopia's new Academy of Pedagogy has attracted international support and attention with several innovations. Its general orientation is to rural development. Its students are required to serve a full year in some prescribed rural service. They are to undertake simple practice research in education and work with faculty in revising public school curriculums and producing teaching materials.

Several developing countries are trying out solutions to teacher shortages: Brazil makes teacher training mandatory for all girls in secondary and higher education; Kenya gives free training to teachers; and several other countries offer special salary scales and rural differentials to attract teachers to undesirable posts.

Exploiting New Instructional Technology

Adoption of new technology has become almost synonymous with innovation in public discussion of remedies for education's major ills. The notion may be justified if technology is defined loosely to include all the physical tools used to facilitate learning plus all the practices used in association with teaching and learning aids. In this discussion, however, "new technology" refers simply to equipment and instructional and managerial techniques for using television, radio, films, language laboratories, and programmed learning systems. These tools seem to have great potential for contributing to the relief of the educational problems of the low-income countries. Realizing their potential, however, has proved far more difficult than early enthusiasts expected.

The primary value of the new devices is their ability to economize on the scarcest resource, good teachers, and trans-

mit high quality educational content to large numbers of learners. They should be able to add realism and excitement to
what for many school inmates is a spiritless and uninspiring
process. They seem to promise productivity gains comparable
to those technology has brought in other fields—speeding the
rate of learning, freeing teachers to devote more time to individualized guidance, bringing the real world into the classroom and relating it to academic disciplines, extending the
reach of an educational system to remote areas and to learners
not in formal schools, reviving interest among potential school
dropouts, helping to reduce inequalities in learning opportunity, and stimulating the pace of educational reform.

Of course these magic lantern promises have several catches.
The educational contribution of these new communications
devices can be no better than the material they convey and the
way they are used. Each device has its limitations and costs.
All depend on expert programming and on the close collaboration of classroom teachers, who must be trained to use them
and who must alter their lesson plans to complement the elec-
tronic teaching. Some teachers resent or fear the intrusion of
these costly competitors. Mechanical maintenance is difficult,
sometimes undependable. Retention of the lesson material by
the student requires planned and supervised action rather
than passive monitoring.

Costs and cost-effectiveness of the new technology have not
yet been fully determined for low-income countries. Because
the new devices do not replace the teacher in a primary or secondary school,[19] they do not lower educational budgets, although they may improve cost-effectiveness. They can provide
a partial substitute for schooling to those now denied any.

19. A narrowly trained classroom monitor can relieve a teacher of some
roles. But a school committed to inculcating positive values and attitudes
toward learning may find it necessary to put its best teachers in the same
grades where instructional television is used.

Mass-audience use of radio and circulated audio-visual materials is relatively inexpensive, but even this expense looms large in a budget in which less than 5 percent is allocated to instructional materials. While efficiency improves with mass applications, the early-years cost of expert programming and operation of an instructional television scheme with all the necessary curriculum revisions and teacher retraining imposes a sharp increase on already pinched school budgets.

Schools have invested increasingly in audio-visual equipment for supplemental or enrichment uses, but there have been many reports of low utilization and dissatisfaction. The common complaint is that the materials are of mediocre quality or take too much class time for the few salient points they convey.

It may be that improving educational quality will be difficult and costly, whatever the methods used. The help that technology can offer may be worth the cost. One observer of the new technology in both developed and less developed countries remains confident after several balanced surveys that it will be a boon to all.[20] Yet a U.S. Commission on Instructional Technology could offer only tentative judgments on many of the questions and doubts its study exposed.[21] The commission found it necessary, because of the rapid growth in this field, to have more than a hundred papers prepared by specialists in addition to reviewing nearly as many already published studies.

In educational technology, as in other fields of development,

20. Wilbur Schramm, "The New Media: Memo to Educational Planner" (Paris: UNESCO, 1967; processed). See also: Wilbur Schramm, "The New Educational Technology," in *Essays on World Education*, pp. 133–52.

21. *To Improve Learning—A Report to the President and the Congress of the United States*, Prepared by the Commission on Instructional Technology for the House Committee on Education and Labor, 91 Cong. 2 sess.(1970).

more carefully designed, monitored, and evaluated pilot projects are needed. While they may be useful in themselves to the community served, they must be conducted so as to yield good measurements of resource requirements and educational results. The design and support of such a matrix of experimental projects should be undertaken by the new U.S. technical assistance agency, in close communication with other agencies active in similar experiments. Several experimental projects that meet these conditions are under way.

El Salvador completed in 1970 the second year of its system-wide experiment in the use of instructional television as the leading feature of a general educational modernization. Its government saw television as one answer to the familiar problems of a developing country struggling with mounting costs of low-output education. The scheme, supported partially by an AID loan and grant, includes curriculum and classroom method revision, teacher retraining, teacher-advisory services, new instructional materials and remodeled classrooms, initial and progress testing, and continuing research. It started with seventh grade classes, then added eighth and ninth grades, in both public and private schools, and may expand to the primary and higher secondary levels if funds are available.

Evaluation of the initial results of using the new curriculum with instructional television showed significant gains in learning in the three subjects measured—science, mathematics, and social studies.[22] It was not possible after the first two years to isolate the effects of television from other elements of the new system. Several more years of experience were considered necessary to measure the effectiveness of the whole reform.

Ivory Coast is trying to make major gains in both the coverage and quality of primary education through a comprehensive

22. Institute for Communications Research, "Television and Educational Reform in El Salvador," Research Report No. 3 (Stanford University, May 1970; processed).

reform built around the use of instructional television. Its ten-year program, launched in 1970 with World Bank, French, and UNESCO/UNDP aid, calls for four television periods of fifteen minutes each day in the first four years of primary school and two periods thereafter. Collateral actions include daily tele-lessons for teachers, as part of a broader teacher training and retraining scheme, plus redesign of the curriculum, more and better instructional materials, smaller class sizes, and automatic promotion.

Planners of the Ivory Coast scheme predict it will double the primary schools' efficiency by radically reducing the number of dropouts and repeaters and by shortening the time required to meet the standards of a primary school-leaving certificate by a year. These savings would more than justify the predicted 9 percent increase in recurrent costs attributed to television when the system is in full operation about the end of this decade.[23] These gains depend in part on the quality and effective integration of television materials into classwork and the attitude of parents toward keeping children in school.

Other instructional television projects, in Niger, Colombia, Samoa, and elsewhere, were begun without establishing the baseline data needed to test their educational effectiveness against alternative methods. As trail-blazers, however, they have provided valuable guidance to the newer, more comprehensive and experimentally designed schemes.

It is apparent that the problem of unqualified or incompetent classroom teachers does not go away when television appears on the scene, at least not at the primary and secondary levels where average students are involved. On the contrary, the studio and classroom teachers must be trained and retrained and their lesson plans continually made more interde-

23. International Bank for Reconstruction and Development, Economic Development Institute, "Ivory Coast ITV Project," staff paper (Washington: IBRD, 1970; processed).

pendent. Without this integrated approach, a school system trying televised or hand-delivered filmed lessons may be able to supplement or enrich its programs but it will not get a bargain in terms of improved educational efficiency.

If this conclusion is justified, it raises tough questions for advocates of satellite transmission of instructional material to vast numbers of schools in big countries or groups of countries. Integration of the studio and classroom teaching will be extremely difficult where authority is decentralized, as in a large country with a federal system, or where different curricula are provided for various language or ethnic groups or for rural and urban schools. Planning of the proposed large-scale experiments with satellite transmission of daily instructional periods in India and Brazil must deal with this problem, among others. Of course, mass audience delivery of educational programs may be worth the cost as a supplement to formal schooling and as a broadside effort in nonformal community education.

Nonformal Vocational and Subprofessional Training

If development policy matures in a rational way in the 1970s, some of the most promising educational innovations will occur outside the formal school systems. There, in a poorly charted outer region called nonformal education, the bulk of man's skills, knowledge, and attitudes are acquired and continually adjusted. More deliberate and logical organization of these processes should yield even higher benefits to the developing countries than they evidently offer the more educationally advanced societies.

Nonformal education means organized and deliberate efforts outside the conventional schools to prepare people for employment or to develop the skills and knowledge of those already employed. It usually is directed at particular subgroups in the present or potential labor force. This large universe includes work-related literacy training, on-the-job or "sand-wiched" training and apprenticeship, agricultural extension, rural training center and young farmer programs, aspects of community development, industrial training provided by equipment suppliers, managerial staff training, government staff training (of teachers, health workers, and population, nutrition, or other program workers in special courses), continuing education offered to the public by schools after regular hours, labor union craft training, correspondence courses using mail, radio, or television, and myriad other activities.

The demand for nonformal education in countries with highly developed formal systems is enormous, supporting the view that "much of the expenditure on education will be wasted unless it is followed up by intensive and systematic training in the course of employment."[24] Nonformal educational expenditures in the United States, while not fully measured, may be approaching the scale of formal educational outlays.[25] Some U.S. industrial corporations operate training establishments as large as the national universities of many countries.

The demand for nonformal education in less developed countries is for both basic and follow-up education. For the millions who will never attend school or go beyond a few grades and other millions whose schooling is poorly related to their or the nation's development, nonformal vocational and literacy training offers a second chance. If it can be made cost-efficient and largely dependent on its beneficiaries for financial support, it offers a "second chance" to governments as well.

Its potential has been only dimly perceived, even in countries where some types of nonformal education have become

24. Frederick Harbison, "The Prime Movers of Innovation," in C. Arnold Anderson and Mary Jean Bowman (eds.), *Education and Economic Development* (Aldine, 1965), p. 238.

25. AID, unpublished staff paper, 1970.

important social institutions. Many have tried to formalize vocational education, making it a poorly performed function of conventional schools, while neglecting the potential for more realistic vocational training through apprenticeship, work–study arrangements, young farmer training on the farm, and specialized technician training tied into job experience. The debate over the right balance between vocational schooling and on-the-job training and between vocation-oriented instruction and general education will continue. Developing countries, however, need both better general education and more efficient specific means of raising the productivity of their greatest resource, manpower, with least increase in recurrent budgets. Apart from economic development, they need nonformal education to build bridges across the social chasm between their "educated" minority and "uneducated" majority. The structure and content of formal education also may bend to examples set by experimental, tradition-free systems of nonformal training.

"Ideal" nonformal models are yet to be invented. No single approach will fit the great variety of potential functions, local styles, and capacities. However, some common criteria for gauging the effectiveness of nonformal training programs can be established. Such programs should exploit the greater realism and learning stimuli of actual employment by offering as much of their training as practicable in real or replicated job sites, using skilled workers or farmers as teaching aides. Work-related functional literacy should be taught as an integral part of job training where needed. Wherever possible, financial support should be sought outside the education ministry budget, in other government agencies (especially in their staff training allocations) but particularly among industrial employers, farmer and labor organizations, local communities, and the trainees themselves. Existing facilities of government, industry, community associations, schools, or farms should be used in order to minimize demand for new buildings, equipment, and logistical and administrative systems.

Some of these conditions are met by the well-established training programs of INCE in Venezuela, SENA in Colombia, SENAI and SENAC in Brazil, and Thailand's Mobile Trade Training Units. Uganda's Extension Saturation Program, Tanzania's Village Polytechnics, and Mexico's Social Security Institute training schemes offer other models for international adaptation. A transplanted concept that may suggest means of drawing education and the local community closer together is the Reverend Leon Sullivan's "opportunity industrialization center" scheme. These centers, in Nigeria and Ghana, engage local enterprises, labor, and government in financing, staffing, and guiding vocational and related social education aimed at known job opportunities.

Assistance to nonformal training plans that meet the suggested criteria should have a much stronger priority in U.S. programs than support of conventional, school-bound vocational education. Techniques used in U.S. industry and in some military programs that emphasize civil skills may be particularly applicable; personnel from these sources may also be better able than those from advanced educational institutions to aid in technical assistance.

Postsecondary Education for Development

The perennial demand for change in "higher education" in the developing countries is that it be designed to produce young men and women equipped for "strategic occupations"[26] and dedicated to the cause of economic and social moderniza-

26. F. Harbison and C. A. Myers, *Education, Manpower and Economic Growth* (McGraw-Hill, 1964), identify the strategic occupations in most developing countires.

tion. Critics of postsecondary education maintain that poor countries can afford to invest in higher education for the fortunate few only to achieve important social or national development goals, and that too much of what goes on in higher education and too large a proportion of its output is irrelevant to or not committed to the tasks of development.

Educational reform—certainly foreign technical assistance —can hardly play a major role in making postsecondary education yield social benefits commensurate with its high social cost. The primary factors that determine who gets the privilege of higher education and what use students and professors make of the privilege are cultural value systems and economic and psychological incentives. Prerequisite to the effective reform of higher education is a change in market demand for its services and products. Such changes seem to be occurring in the natural course of political and economic evolution, particularly in the rapid growth of public responsibility for social services. Technical assistance can contribute to this change by expanding the market for problem-oriented researchers, innovative managers, and technical manpower.

Technical assistance can continue to help in adapting professional or higher technical education to local needs. Over the past ten to fifteen years, U.S. assistance to agricultural colleges, medical schools, teacher training colleges, institutes of development administration, and engineering, science, and technology departments or schools has attempted to steer higher education away from the less practical or more cloistered academic fields.

Recent manpower bottlenecks in scientific agricultural development and in health, population, and other expanding social services have made it urgent to channel more students and resources into specialized postsecondary training below the university level. International assistance agencies have been uncertain, passive, unimaginative in their response to these needs. A program of U.S. assistance based on opportunities for innovative assistance in those sectors would make a better policy than generalized support for establishing or "strengthening higher education."

Assistance should be concentrated on specific functional fields, on needed changes in those fields that can be made by particular educational actions. For example, resources for medical education should go into training and indoctrinating doctors and paramedical or auxiliary personnel for community medicine and into moving the teaching of community medicine actively into field operations and research. Support for agricultural programs should attempt to link higher education with research and extension or to strengthen economics or other weak teaching areas of a nation's agricultural higher education. Assistance should be given to efforts to integrate faculties of economics, business administration, social studies, and public administration in order to provide teaching programs and research in national development analysis and management. Encouragement should be given innovators with workable schemes to make teacher education reform-oriented and to build research, development, and extension programs into higher education. Conversion of schools of engineering and departments of economics into composite institutions or programs for training capital project analysts and managers for either public or private development work should be sought. Universities should be offered visiting professors, "endowed" chairs, research grants or funds, and overseas study grants to enable them to add strong courses in demography, fertility control, nutrition, and other neglected fields to their general and professional curricula, economics to their medical curricula, and so on.

These examples of a policy of specificity in postsecondary education assistance are ambitious. But taken in digestible bites, they avoid some of the risks and uncertainties of trying to create and nurture to maturity a whole new "development university" or a complete model for reform of professional and technical education.

Summary

The educational dilemmas of developing countries cry out for imaginative, low-cost solutions. Despite great efforts and impressive achievements, education at every level continues to fall short of meeting either social demand for equal opportunity or developmental demand for adequately prepared manpower. Traditional educational systems have proved too wasteful of scarce resources for countries struggling on every front against poverty, population pressures, and time.

In the 1970s the developing countries will be forced by budgetary limitations and dissatisfaction with their educational output to intensify the search for better ways of using limited educational resources. Among the reforms begun in the 1960s, the best hope lies in technological innovation—not machines alone, or even primarily, but tools and techniques of organizing learning processes for greater output within the means of low-income countries. The needs for innovation range from school management and educational finance to teacher preparation and augmentation, curriculum and structural reform, and exploitation of learning opportunities and facilities outside the formal educational systems.

While each country's values and political system must determine the design and execution of its educational reforms, international cooperation can accelerate problem solving and minimize duplication of costly trial and error. International assistance should concentrate on reinforcing the trailblazers through professional collaboration and financial support to innovative programs and operations-oriented research, rather than giving what can only be marginal support to traditional educational systems.

The virtual lack of national networks (or of strong international reinforcement) linking educational research with experimental programs, educator training, and "extension services" to school administrators and teachers should be attacked primarily by using technical assistance to strengthen market demand for problem-solving research and creative ideas.

The opportunities should thus be wider and more challenging for U.S. educational experts and institutions to work directly with the developing countries and with international intermediaries. Among the promising opportunities are comprehensive sectoral analysis and planning, refinement and extension of reforms in formal educational systems, nonformal vocational and subprofessional training innovations, use of new instructional technologies, and teacher training. The latter three clusters should get higher priority than the others in U.S. technical assistance. Deliberate efforts should be made to utilize the extensive U.S. knowledge and experience in industrial, agricultural, and other training systems outside the formal educational community.

Professional and subprofessional manpower development for agriculture, industry, health, nutrition, and population programs should be integral parts of technical assistance to those sectors. No longer can U.S. technical assistance be devoted to generalized support of higher education; it must instead be targeted on particular institutional changes aimed at bringing professional and subprofessional training into closer and more efficient association with research and operations in each field.

CHAPTER EIGHT

Putting It All Together

ALMOST EVERY low-income country desperately needs radically better ways of using scarce resources in six fundamental, interdependent fields—agriculture, industry, health, nutrition, population, and education. Together, those areas pose the main challenges to international technical cooperation in the 1970s.

This study has concentrated on those aspects of technical assistance where demand for U.S. assistance is widespread and U.S. innovative capacity is clearly relevant to the circumstances of Asia, Africa, and Latin America. Technical assistance functions primarily performed by capital finance agencies and increasingly addressed by the World Bank and International Monetary Fund were deliberately excluded.

Traditionally, capital finance agencies or development banks were limited to making preinvestment surveys, feasibility studies, and procurement recommendations, and offering advisory services (including occasional expatriate staff reinforcement) to intermediate credit institutions. As comprehensive economic planning and broad financial support of national or sectoral growth plans became prominent features of development cooperation, the international lending agencies became interested in the development policies and institutions of borrower countries. Concessional lending for development could not sensibly ignore the relationship between the need for and use of external resources and the borrower's performance in mobilization of domestic fiscal or financial resources, however politically sensitive the issue might be. Multilateral banks can be more acceptable and professional intervenors in internal fiscal and financial affairs than can national agencies.

The international banks have a concomitant obligation to intervene in the problems of economic management in developing countries. The best plans and the most professional advisory consultations will avail little if the organs responsible for executing the plans are inadequate. The banks should not simply refuse to lend in such cases but should help in institution building, with staff training, systems analysis, and specialized management services, and if necessary with expatriate staff. Technical assistance grants sometimes are necessary to get action on human resource investments of this sort. There is no logical reason for the regional or international development banks to dodge responsibility on this account.

Perspective

The foregoing review of experience and of needs for technical assistance in the six fundamental fields indicates the absolute necessity for greater cost-effectiveness in public service programs, an efficiency higher in some respects than has been required in the wealthier countries where neither population pressures nor the accumulation of unmet social demand is nearly as severe as in the poor nations. Public service programs are often insensitive to the real demands of their markets; the market signals for guiding these programs need to be strengthened in every field. Technology is so critically important in bringing about progress in nearly every field that international cooperation must aim at accelerating the creation and adaptation of technologies to serve the developing countries. Concurrent, equally imaginative changes must be made in social organizations and policies to assure that technological innovations are both effective and broadly beneficial to the disadvantaged majorities.

For both the developing countries and the international assistance community there are risks as well as great benefits in technological modernization. Some latter-day Luddites and intellectual champions of the simple life would have the less developed countries remain in that condition, shunning the risks of change. "Why don't they stick with the old ways of subsistence farming?" they ask. "Why do they need to go into manufacturing (and compete with us)?" "Why should they give up the joys and security of many children?" "Don't they only achieve frustration through more education?"

The facts and projections summarized in this study make clear that the vast majority of the world's people simply have no possibility of coping with their accelerating demand for jobs, food, or income to support the most basic social services and investment, nor of satisfying their aspirations for better health and nutrition and education for their children unless they harness the power of technology to raise the value of their labor, capital, land, and other natural resources. The technologies they need have little to do with the caricatured "dehumanizing machines." They are high-yielding and high-protein varieties of staple food crops; means of controlling plant and animal diseases; defenses against poverty-rooted human afflictions; low-cost means of extending the delivery of health, nutrition, and fertility-control services; contraceptive technologies adapted to the circumstances of poor societies; capital-saving industrial processes; new systems of organizing basic and vocational education and producing strategic subprofessional manpower at tolerable cost; and a host of other technological innovations that when coupled with social innovations can profoundly benefit humanity.

Technological change will, indeed, bring new social and economic problems. Rising productivity can outrace new employment opportunities and disrupt traditional systems that protect the marginal producer. Declining mortality intensifies population pressures before it induces changes in the social norms that encourage high birth rates. Expanding agricultural and industrial production is frustrated when domestic or export markets are restricted. Training for jobs is an expensive ticket to nowhere if jobs are not created fast enough.

These are ways of saying that development is a circular process, and it usually takes more than the "invisible hand" of classical economic theory to assure that the social gains of technological innovation exceed social costs. Providing the required foresight and correctives is an important function of development strategies. Yet, in most of the developing countries there are, almost by definition, acute shortages of knowledge, skills, institutions, or vision required to design, blend, and manage social and technological innovations.

The broad tasks of international technical assistance are to enable the developing countries to reduce these critical gaps in their analytical and problem-solving capacities and to improve their means of exploiting their resources advantageously. This is not a one-year or even one-decade task. The approaches to it, however, do need periodic reassessment and adjustment to evolving demand and opportunity.

A Program for the Seventies

The lessons of two decades of experience and the key problems common to many developing countries point to the desirable evolution of U.S. technical assistance in the years ahead. In the main, the new directions lie in systematic, operations-oriented research, in research-disciplined experimental projects, and in a less tutelary, more collaborative set of professional relationships in all aspects of technical cooperation.

The administrators of U.S. technical assistance should focus more sharply on the fundamental human problems common to many less developed countries, and the United States should specialize in areas where its strong comparative advantage has been proven and where U.S. professional involvement is politically acceptable to the developing countries. The specific suggestions offered in the six sectoral discussions amount to an effort to revitalize U.S. technical assistance by making it more relevant to the problem-solving needs of development, more attractive to a new generation of American experts, and more likely to engage the talents of professional people and institutions in the developing countries.

A collaborative style in technical cooperation is fundamental. The market for old-fashioned "show and tell" advice by U.S. government employees is declining in the developing countries as their nationalism and self-confidence increase. Yet they still need—some of them desperately—more expert manpower than they have been able to train, retain, and mobilize locally. Their professional communities still welcome collaboration with foreign experts, but the professionals are not adequately engaged in the systems dealing with key development problems. The politics of many developing countries tend to alienate both local and American experts. In order to mobilize this talent, development administration must foster professional programs that appeal to humanitarian and sectoral interests. Joint research, experimental projects, and training programs, both national and multinational, are particularly suited to such professional collaboration. Americans should participate, wherever practicable, under the auspices of nongovernmental institutions or as individuals and be fully integrated in local staffs or joint teams.

Engaging the Best Talent

There are four standard ways of engaging expert manpower in publicly supported technical assistance work: direct staffing of an official aid agency, such as the UN specialized agencies or the U.S. technical assistance agency; borrowing of individuals or teams from domestic public agencies such as the U.S. Agricultural Research Service, the Public Health Service, or the Census Bureau; contracting, usually between an aid-receiving government and a foreign company or university; and supplementary financing of the programs of private or quasi-private institutions such as the Population Council, the international agricultural research institutes, regional development bodies, or professional associations. The execution of technical cooperation in projects supported by U.S. official assistance should be almost entirely in the hands of experts and institutions other than the technical assistance agency, that is, through use of "professional intermediaries."

The decision to rely in U.S. programs on professional intermediaries rests on the somewhat questionable assumption that top-quality talent is or can quickly be pooled in the existing firms, agencies, and institutes, in the numbers required, for all the important technical fields in which the United States has comparative strength and there is demand for technical assistance. Moreover, it is assumed that all the intermediary organizations and their personnel are readily adaptable to the social, physical, or lingual environments of developing countries and adjustable to a collaborative kind of role. In fact, there are gaps in the subject-area and geographic competence of the firms and quasi-private organizations available for contracting or capable of conducting their own programs. Even the largest firms, domestic public agencies, and foundations frequently are unable to provide qualified staff for urgently requested services to developing countries. Broad-gauge and adaptable team leaders are particularly scarce. Some organizations require official administrative support or fiscal or substantive surveillance that negates their independent, nongovernmental character in their overseas relationships.

Curing these weaknesses in the actual capacity to perform effectively will be a continuing challenge to both the managers of the U.S. technical assistance program and the professional communities concerned. It will not be enough to appeal for expert participation in the programs and to promise long-term demand for professional services. If actual, specific demand continues to be uncertain and erratic, an intermediary institution will be unable to keep superior talent on tap. Nor can a large part of U.S. technical assistance funds be spent in maintaining standby capacity in intermediary organizations or keeping private program staffs fully employed; the U.S. program managers would lose control of their priorities and the developing countries would be short-changed.

Reconciliation of these interests may be found in a combination of measures:

Technical assistance functions should be built up in special-purpose centers like the international agricultural research centers.

Financial support should be given U.S. centers of excellence that initiate or participate in international collaborative research programs directed at key technological innovations.

Outstanding U.S. universities or other nonprofit institutions should be designated as chosen instruments of U.S. technical assistance for specific functions (for example, fish farming, low-cost basic educational technology, national industrial research management); they should be provided modest research funds to maintain their knowledge of developing country needs and applications of technology; and developing countries should be encouraged to use their services.

In key fields where recruiting problems are chronic, such as agricultural planning, the U.S. technical assistance agency and professional experts should form an association pledged to provide advisers or staff to developing countries; the association should have a small research or study fund to help maintain the members' interest in overseas service and their current knowledge of problems in particular countries or regions.

A similar pool of experts should be created for the social and motivational aspects of population programs; the present informal "club" of university specialists in this field might be institutionalized or given an internationally recognized identity or a consortium of institutions might be formed to assist in research and operational programs. A U.S. association should be established for industrial research experts, composed of retired or independent research managers and specialists who are prepared to serve as short- or medium-term staff members (including managers) of research programs in companies, industrial associations, or public institutions of the developing countries; the association, through U.S. technical assistance financing, could "top off" local salaries and carry on recruiting and orientation of volunteers.

A pool of agricultural research and extension system-designers, possibly centered in the U.S. Agricultural Research Service or in a consortium of land grant colleges or a separate institution, should be considered as a means of improving research management; the U.S. technical assistance program should provide travel and international conference funds to enable the group to maintain common knowledge of effective approaches and conditions in the developing countries and generally spread the concepts of problem-oriented research management. Technical assistance contracts should include funds to enable staff to be trained by intermediaries before they undertake overseas assignments and to write professional papers or do follow-up research on completion of assignments.

A single prime intermediary, such as a group of universities or a large consulting firm, should be designated to handle all U.S. technical assistance in a small and narrowly focused country program. In more advanced developing countries the management of U.S. technical assistance may be wholesaled to bilateral, nonprofit foundations created for this purpose and jointly financed by the two governments; a large part of their outlays for professional work would go to local rather than U.S. researchers.

The UN Development Program and specialized UN agencies should be urged to make greater use of U.S. contractors, again with the objective of assuring a broader demand for U.S. intermediaries as well as raising the quality of UN programs.

The private groups whose participation is essential to a revitalized and more professional U.S. technical assistance program will undoubtedly suggest other ways of attracting and utilizing experts. The main attraction of the program, however, is its nature—the opportunities it offers for significant roles in reducing problems that afflict much of mankind. These are opportunities that suit the American spirit and genius. They provide a means of expressing internationally the best of the U.S. national character—a blend of creativity, practicality, and humanitarian involvement.

A Continuing Renewal

The great challenges to U.S. technical assistance in the 1970s are complex issues demanding sustained technological and social innovation. Both the nature of these issues and the political environment for international action on them call for professional collaboration at several institutional levels, public and private, national and international, rather than the simple donor–recipient relationships of the past. They require all concerned to sharpen their focus on the key problems and to commit to the effort a higher order of professional competence than the average of programs mounted by either Americans or the agencies of the developing countries in the past.

In suggesting steps toward such a renaissance in U.S. technical assistance, this study has stressed the presently perceived new and urgent tasks. Other, unforeseen opportunities will emerge. What is important is to devise better systems for identifying and coping with the critical problems, recognizing that development will continue to be desperately urgent unfinished business for most of the world far into the future.

The United States has, despite its own long experience in international technical assistance, been evading formal, official recognition of the fact that this is a central feature of its relations with the developing nations. Technical cooperation supported by U.S. public funds will continue to be a necessary and desirable role for Americans on the world stage in the 1980s and beyond. It is high time that the United States accept this fact of international life and make technical cooperation a permanent yet constantly renewed commitment of all its professional communities.

Agricultural Research Priorities

A CANVASS of agricultural experts and institutions reveals a high correlation in their suggestions for research priorities
for developing countries. The lists that follow were suggested in
private letters from the individuals designated or, when so stated,
drawn from published papers.

Nyle C. Brady, director of research at Cornell University and
chairman of the Research Advisory Committee of the Agency for
International Development, puts the greatest weight on research
in: tropical soils management; adaptive work on high-yielding crop
varieties, particularly grains, for diverse growing regions; irrigation
and water management; pesticide and biological control of insect
pests and crop diseases; and veterinary medicine for tropical livestock production.

H. F. Robinson, vice chancellor of the University of Georgia and
former executive director of the Panel on the World Food Supply
of the President's Science Advisory Council, suggests these priorities: adaptation of high-yielding grains to the climates, soils, and
pathogens of various environments; breeding of commonly used
cereals for high-protein content; breeding of greater disease resistance into commonly used food crops; soil and water management
for irrigated agriculture, including prevention and mitigation of
salinity.

High Popenoe, director of the Center for Tropical Agriculture,
University of Florida, stresses: genetic improvements and better
production practices for the traditional tropical food crops—sweet
potato, cassava, sago, hasheen, and plantain; cheap means of improving the nitrogen content of tropical pastures, including better
adapted grain legumes; fish farming; improved management prac-

tices that utilize improved seed varieties along with some of the inherent advantages of traditional agriculture, such as multicrop farming, reliance on biological rather than chemical control of pests and diseases, labor intensity, and small holdings; agricultural utilization of estuary and tidal lands; and better methodology for vocational agricultural training.

F. F. Hill, chairman of the Board of Directors of the International Rice Research Institute and member of the Board of the International Institute of Tropical Agriculture, proposes: multiple cropping in the tropics, using high-yielding, season-variable varieties and new production practices; beef cattle production in tropical areas of Latin America; soil management in the humid tropics to permit continuous instead of intermittent use of land without loss of soil productivity; water management in both irrigated and nonirrigated areas of the less developed nations, including field practices, distribution and control of water, land leveling, layout and maintenance of irrigation works, surveys of surface and subsurface water resources, drainage, water rights, and related problems; and regional agricultural economics surveys and services, including training.

A. H. Boerma, director general, Food and Agriculture Organization, United Nations, and staff, in papers submitted to the 1969 Agricultural Development Conference at Bellagio, Italy, suggested: improved cereal varieties suitable for rainfed agriculture; further adaptation of high-yielding cereal varieties to incorporate valuable protective and taste characteristics of local varieties and minimize the risk of wholesale plant disease losses; crop diversification and alternative use of land taken out of cereal crops by countries where high-yielding cereals have been very successful; improvement of high-protein grain legumes and oilseed crops, serving both nutrition and land-rotation objectives; improved varieties and practices for pasture and fodder crop production; unspecified work on vegetables and fruit crops; and adaptation to more environments of high-yielding varieties of cassava, potato, sweet potato, and other tubers.

Sterling Wortman, vice president of the Rockefeller Foundation, gives overriding weight to the whole field of high-yielding technology, for all major food and fiber crops and food-animal species "for every season, in every region of every nation." He emphasizes breeding and practices to produce high yields, stating that rapid increases in production depend on the development and demonstration of "complete packages of technology, adapted to local conditions, which permit two-fold or greater increases in absolute yield."

Participants in the 1970 Agricultural Development Conference at Bellagio, Italy, identified these subjects for research: (1) Cereal crops: rice for upland cultivation in tropical Latin America; wheat for irrigated cultivation in Northeast Africa, for rainfed farming in South Asia, the Near East, and North Africa; millet for South Asia, Northeast Africa, and possible other areas; sorghum for rainfed cultivation in most regions; and maize for rainfed cultivation in monsoon Asia and tropical Africa. (2) Crops other than cereals: groundnuts, soybeans, and grain legumes in virtually all regions; tropical root tubers in tropical Africa and tropical Latin America; plantains in tropical Africa and Latin America; and Irish potatoes in Andean and other high mountain regions. (3) Livestock: tropical bovine breeding, using present fodders, in Africa; bovine fodder research, using present breeds of cattle, in all regions; animal management systems, altering both fodders and breeds, in all regions; pastoral animal management systems in South Asia, the Near East, and North and Northeast Africa; livestock processing and marketing in all regions except temperate and mountainous Latin America. (4) Farm production systems: low rainfall areas of South Asia, the Near East, and North and Northeast Africa; high mountain areas of the Near East, North Africa, and Latin America; shifting cultivation areas of southern Asia and tropical Africa and Latin America; inventory of water resources in southern Asia and, with possibly lower priority, the Near East and North Africa; methods of water exploitation in the Near East, and North and Northeast Africa; methods of on-farm water management in all regions except Latin America and mountainous areas. (5) Loss prevention: grain storage, drying, milling, and processing and rodent control in most regions.

Index

Abel-Smith, B., 114n
Abortion, 117, 121, 132–33, 141.
  See also Contraceptives; Population control
Academy of Pedagogy (Ethiopia), 221
Advanced Institute of Sciences (Korea), 76
Advisory Committee on Tropical Medicine, 111
Africa: agriculture in, 19–20, 26, 46; education in, 198, 201, 205; health care, 92, 105; industry in, 55; population growth, 53. *See also specific country*
Agency for International Development (AID): agricultural research, 20, 43, 45–46; criticism of, 9–11; education funding, 217, 219–20, 224; health assistance, 104, 109; and industrial technology, 63; medical research, 105; nutrition study, 171, 179; origin, 9; and Peterson report, 12; population research, 137, 139, 142; and U.S. Congress, 14. *See also* Technical assistance
Agricultural research: in cereals, 19–24, 46; development administration of, 22–27, 33–39; disease control, 23–24, 29–30; economic effect, 20–22, 32; extension services, 20, 27, 30, 34–35, 43, 201, 231, 241; in fertilizers, 30–31; financing of,

40–48; and food demand, 17–19; in food preservation, 176, 189; in food research, 188–90; international coordination of, 39–47, 240; and nutrition, 26, 172–73, 175–76, 188; origin, 10–11; population variable, 25; priorities in, 28–33; regional centers for, 47–48; soil, 30–32, 38, 43; U.S. and, 25, 231, 241; water management, 21, 30, 32, 38, 44. *See also* Agriculture
Agriculture: economics of, 32–33, 53–54; education in, 26–27, 31; exports, 16; extension services, 20, 27, 30–31, 34–35, 43, 156, 209, 231, 241; farm size, 20–21, 26, 53; need projection, 17–19. *See also* Agricultural research
AID. *See* Agency for International Development
Altschul, Aaron, 175n, 180n
Asia: agriculture in, 19, 46; health care in, 92; industry in, 57; labor productivity, 57; population growth, 53. *See also specific country*
Atlanta, 104
Atta flour, 167, 178–79
Auburn University, 46
Australia, 69

Babayan, S., 159n
Bacillary dysentery, 105
Baer, Werner, 60n

247